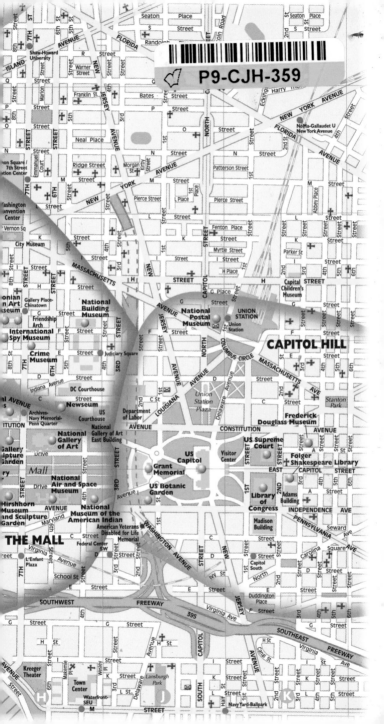

How to Use This Book

KEY TO SYMBOLS	
✚ Map reference to the accompanying fold-out map	⛴ Nearest riverboat or ferry stop
✉ Address	♿ Facilities for visitors with disabilities
☎ Telephone number	❓ Other practical information
🕓 Opening/closing times	▷ Further information
🍴 Restaurant or café	ℹ Tourist information
🚆 Nearest rail station	✋ Admission charges: Expensive (over $9), Moderate ($4–$9), and Inexpensive ($3 or less)
🚇 Nearest Metro (subway) station	
🚌 Nearest bus route	

This guide is divided into four sections

• Essential Washington: An introduction to the city and tips on making the most of your stay.
• Washington by Area: We've broken the city into six areas, and recommended the best sights, shops, entertainment venues, nightlife and restaurants in each one. Suggested walks help you to explore on foot. Farther Afield takes you out of the city.
• Where to Stay: The best hotels, whether you're looking for luxury, budget or something in between.
• Need to Know: The info you need to make your trip run smoothly, including getting about by public transportation, weather tips, emergency phone numbers and useful websites.

Navigation In the Washington by Area chapter, we've given each area its own color, which is also used on the locator maps throughout the book and the map on the inside front cover.

Maps The fold-out map accompanying this book is a comprehensive street plan of Washington. The grid on this fold-out map is the same as the grid on the locator maps within the book. We've given grid references within the book for each sight and listing.

Contents

Introducing Washington

Equal parts Southern gentility, Northern sophistication and power politics, America's capital is a microcosm of the United States, the melting pot's melting pot. Washington DC is both quintessentially American and unique as an American city.

Washington is a city that was founded on politics because it was a compromise from the start. The site was chosen, close to George Washington's home at Mount Vernon, after a deal was brokered for the South to pay the North's revolutionary war debts in exchange for having a southern capital. Virginia and Maryland donated land for the District, and architect Pierre Charles L'Enfant (1754–1825) designed a city with a focal triangle formed by the Capitol, the president's house and a statue where the Washington Monument now sits.

L'Enfant also included plans for the Mall and wide diagonal boulevards crossing the grid of streets. L'Enfant's magnificent vision can be appreciated now, but for a long time this city was little more than a sparsely populated swamp with empty avenues. Cattle grazed on the Mall and America's famous early leaders inhabited and worked in dank, dilapidated buildings.

This city is rich in things to see. Capitol Hill and the Mall, replete with free museums, galleries and monuments, exhibit the magnificence of America's wealth and artistry. The revitalized U Street and Columbia Heights reveal its cultural dynamism. Embassies have brought foreign delegations and friends, imbuing this relatively small city with pockets of cuisine and culture unavailable elsewhere in the US. And the arts scene, in part fueled by the droves of young professionals that move to the capital clamoring for powerful positions, is sophisticated.

But although different types of businesses are moving to the city and helping to invigorate it, its core business remains government.

FACTS AND FIGURES

- The 230ft (70m) escalator at the Wheaton Metro station, in Montgomery County, is the longest in the Western Hemisphere.
- The Pentagon, at 6.6 million sq ft (613,000sq m), is the world's third largest building by floor area and has nearly 17.5 miles (28.2km) of corridors and 131 stairways.

TAXATION, REPRESENTATION?

Washington DC license plates read "Taxation without Representation," a familiar refrain from the Revolutionary War. In this case the term alludes to the fact that the District lacks a voting representative in Congress. To add insult to injury, the Constitution also specifically gives Congress control over Washington's entire budget.

DC ON FIRE

On August 25, 1814, as part of the ongoing War of 1812, British soldiers entered Washington and began torching the town. They destroyed many buildings, including the Capitol and the White House, but not before dining on a feast First Lady Dolley Madison hubristically prepared before being forced to leave. Both buildings still retain scars from the incident.

SECOND SUBWAY

Members of Congress in a rush to vote need not break a sweat. In 1909, underground subway cars were installed to traverse the little more than 500ft (150m) between the Russell Senate Office Building and the Capitol. As subsequent office buildings were added, so were more train lines. These cars, most still open-top, continue to operate today.

A Short Stay in Washington

DAY 1

Morning Start your day at **Union Station** (▷ 68) and grab some coffee in the food court or a more substantial breakfast at the café in the main hall. Follow the flood of "Hill staffers" (▷ 123) as they head to work just before 9am. Most of them will stop at the Senate Office Buildings. You should, too, if you have arranged a tour in advance. Otherwise head to the Capitol Visitor Center at the **Capitol** (▷ 60). Take a tour of the Capitol.

Lunch Head west out of the Capitol and onto the Mall. Either enjoy a meal of Native American delicacies at the **National Museum of the American Indian** (▷ 44) or lunch at the Cascade café, with a view of the waterfall, at the **National Gallery of Art** (▷ 43).

Afternoon Stay on after lunch and take in an exhibit at either museum, neither of which will disappoint.

Mid-afternoon Walk west along the Mall past the Smithsonian museums to the **Washington Monument** (▷ 46). Head up to the top (it's best to reserve tickets in advance) to catch a spectacular view of the city. On coming back down to earth walk due north to **The White House** (▷ 25).

Dinner Walk up to Farragut North Metro station and take the train downtown to the Gallery Place–Chinatown Metro station. Head west on G Street for Mediterranean tapas at the light, airy and lively **Zaytinya** (▷ 32).

Evening After dinner, grab drinks at **Rosa Mexicano** (▷ 32) or **La Tasca** (▷ 30) before taking in a show at the **Shakespeare Theatre** (▷ 30) or **Woolly Mammoth** (▷ 30), depending on whether you like the Bard or avant garde.

DAY 2

Morning Start off the day at the **National Zoological Park** (▷ 84). Be sure to say hello to the panda, the orangutans on the "O line" and the Komodo dragon, the first to be born outside of Indonesia.

Mid-morning Walk south on Connecticut Avenue and hop on the Metro to **Dupont Circle** (▷ 88). Or, if you made it a short stay at the zoo, walk across the Calvert Street Bridge and take an immediate right down 18th Street through **Adams-Morgan** (▷ panel, 92).

Lunch If it's warm, try one of the outdoor cafés near the Metro's north entrance or on 17th Street, or take a picnic to the Circle. There are also many good indoor options on Connecticut Avenue north and south of the Circle, and on P Street west of the Circle.

Afternoon Take the Metro to the Smithsonian station. Walk toward the **Washington Monument** (▷ 46) to 15th Street SW and take a left, heading toward the Tidal Basin, where you will find the **FDR** and **Jefferson memorials** (▷ 36).

Mid-afternoon Walk from the FDR Memorial north to the Reflecting Pool and the **Lincoln Memorial** (▷ 38), where Martin Luther King, Jr. delivered his "I Have a Dream" speech in 1963.

Dinner Enjoy the carefully crafted food at the restaurants in the **Mandarin Oriental hotel** (▷ 112): **Muze** (▷ 52) if you want to go all out or the Empress Lounge if you're looking for something more casual.

Evening Catch a taxi to the **John F. Kennedy Center** (▷ 74), where, depending on the night, you can choose between ballet, opera, the symphony and world-class theater, among other things.

Top 25

►►►

ESSENTIAL WASHINGTON TOP 25

Arlington National Cemetery ▷ 98–99 National heroes, like JFK, are buried here.

FDR and Jefferson Memorials ▷ 36 Two beautiful memorials to two revered statesmen.

Frederick Douglass NHS ▷ 100 The former home of the anti-slavery abolitionist Frederick Douglass.

The White House ▷ 25 This icon is both the president's home and his office.

Washington National Cathedral ▷ 87 This Gothic cathedral is the sixth largest in the world and has held state funerals.

Washington Monument ▷ 46–47 Windows in the top of this iconic obelisk offer panoramic city views.

Vietnam Veterans Memorial ▷ 48 A powerful memorial to the soldiers killed and missing in action in Vietnam.

US Supreme Court Building ▷ 63 An austere building where monumental cases are decided.

US Holocaust Memorial Museum ▷ 45 An unforgettable memorial to the millions exterminated by the Nazis in World War II.

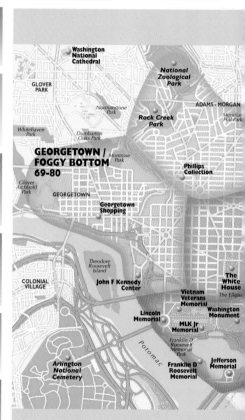

US Capitol ▷ 60–61 Important debates of the day rage under this famous dome, which is also a showcase of Americana.

US Botanic Garden ▷ 58–59 This elegant conservatory houses tropical and subtropical plants from around the world.

Rock Creek Park ▷ 86 This wooded gorge in the heart of Washington DC is popular with hikers, bikers and joggers.

These pages are a quick guide to the Top 25, which are described in more detail later. Here they are listed alphabetically, and the tinted background shows which area they are in.

Freer and Arthur M. Sackler Galleries ▷ 37 Some of the finest Asian art in the West.

Georgetown Shopping ▷ 73 DC's rich and powerful live and shop amid these tree-lined streets.

International Spy Museum ▷ 24 Learn about espionage through history at this fun museum.

John F. Kennedy Center ▷ 74 Washington's premier performing arts center; world-class performances.

Library of Congress ▷ 57 Jefferson's former collection is now a temple to the written word.

Lincoln Memorial ▷ 38 A somber monument to a complicated president.

Martin Luther King, Jr. Memorial ▷ 39 A fitting tribute to the American civil rights leader, set within parkland.

National Air and Space Museum ▷ 40–41 Soaring displays trace the progress of man reaching for the stars.

National Archives ▷ 42 America's scrapbook offers a first-hand peek at history.

National Gallery of Art ▷ 43 A treasure house of European and American art.

National Museum of the American Indian ▷ 44 Educational exhibits on America's first inhabitants.

Phillips Collection ▷ 85 Renowned collection of modern art in Phillips's Georgian revival mansion.

National Zoological Park ▷ 84 The public's park is home to more than 2,000 animals from more than 400 species.

Map labels

NORTHWEST WASHINGTON 81–94

Brentwood Park

DOWNTOWN 20–32

OWNTOWN
ranklin Park

TRINIDAD

International Spy Museum

STANTON PARK

CAPITOL HILL 53–68

Stanton Park

National Archives

National Gallery of Art

US Capitol

US Supreme Court

CAPITOL HILL

Lincoln Park

eer and rthur M Sackler alleries

The Mall

US Botanic Garden

Library of Congress

s Holocaust emorial useum

National Air and Space Museum

National Museum of the American Indian

THE MALL 33–52

Frederick Douglass National Historic Site

◀ ◀ ◀

ESSENTIAL WASHINGTON TOP 25

9

Shopping

For those who see Washington as a wonky, button-down city, the abundance of DC shopping options, from high-end showrooms to chic boutiques, might come as a surprise. Those with style and the money to prove it will find shops like Chanel, Tiffany and Co. and Louis Vuitton in Friendship Heights and Chevy Chase. Vintage hunters can rummage for deals along the Adams-Morgan strip, on U Street or in Eastern Market on Capitol Hill. Mainstreamers will find solace in their favorite stores Downtown, in Georgetown and Pentagon City. Antiques and art hounds should head to Georgetown or Dupont Circle. Hip hard-to-find styles for body and home can be found on Book Hill in Georgetown and on U Street.

Bookworms

This city has not shortchanged its inordinate number of policy experts, think tanks and foundations with a lack of reading material. You'll find two major chains—Barnes and Noble and Books-a-Million—are well-represented, but bookworms will also find some unbeatable independents, such as Kramerbooks and Politics & Prose, that often include comfortable cafés and reading areas among their eclectic collections. Specialty shops—including those that cater to gays and lesbians, history buffs and experts, among countless others—are also abundant.

Broaden the Mind

In fact, DC is generally the place to go if you're looking for something to broaden your mind.

PATTERNS FROM AFRICA

You may be intrigued by the vibrant colors and patterns of the kente cloth clothing worn by chic African-Americans in DC. Hand-woven in Ghana, it's available in bolts to sew with or made up into outfits from several good sources. Start your search at the National Museum of African Art (☎ 202/633–4600).

Georgetown (top and middle) and the window display of the French Market (bottom)

Aside from being a visual cornucopia for students of any age, the city's many museums and galleries contain gift shops and bookstores that extend the experience and learning process. The National Museum of the American Indian stocks an expansive collection of Native American crafts, games and books. The National Building Museum carries a huge library of books on DC and the building arts. Many art museums around town, including the National Gallery of Art and the Hirshhorn, sell items ranging from exhibit catalogs to artisanal jewelry and high-quality prints. The National Air and Space Museum carries glow-in-the-dark stars and freeze-dried astronaut food. And the National Museum of Natural History stocks everything from beautiful housewares to science kits for all ages.

Memorabilia

Likewise, nearly every government building and monument—including the White House, the Capitol, the Library of Congress and the Lincoln Memorial—sells American memorabilia.

Regional Delights

Washington is a good place to buy food and household items sourced from the surrounding regions: Virginia peanuts, ham from North Carolina, Virginia and Kentucky, Pennsylvania quilts and Appalachian handicrafts such as handmade brooms and corn-husk dolls.

Georgetown (top); Chanel store (top middle); fresh crabs (middle); stylish shoes (bottom)

POLITICAL EPHEMERA

Election year or not, DC is a ready source of campaign ephemera—buttons, bumper stickers, matchbooks with party logos and the like. At bookstores, museum gift shops and street vendors, reproductions and original memorabilia abound. Looking for pewter flatware and candlesticks used by 18th-century administrations? A tacky T-shirt commenting on the latest Washington scandal? Who can resist the salt and pepper shakers shaped like the Washington Monument or campaign buttons designed for FDR? For this kind of Americana, there's no place like DC.

Shopping by Theme

Whether you're looking for a department store, a quirky boutique, or something in between, you'll find it all in Washington. On this page shops are listed by theme. For a more detailed write-up, see the individual listings in Washington by Area.

Art and Antiques
Claude Taylor
    Photography (▷ 90)
Good Wood (▷ 90)
Hemphill Fine Arts
    (▷ 90)
Jean Pierre Antiques
    (▷ 77)
National Gallery of Art
    (▷ 52)
The Old Print Gallery
    (▷ 77)
Torpedo Factory Art
    Center (▷ 104)

Books
Bridge Street Books
    (▷ 77)
Capitol Hill Books (▷ 66)
Kramerbooks (▷ 90)
Reiter's Books (▷ 29)
Second Story Books
    (▷ 91)

Food and Wine
A. Litteri (▷ 66)
Calvert Woodley Liquors
    (▷ 90)
Dean and Deluca (▷ 80)
Eastern Market (▷ 64, 66)

For Kids
Dawn Price Baby (▷ 66)
Fairy Godmother (▷ 66)
National Air and Space
    Museum (▷ 52)
National Museum of
    the American Indian
    (▷ 52)
National Museum of
    Natural History (▷ 52)

Home Furnishings
A Mano (▷ 77)
Anthropologie (▷ 77)
Bed Bath & Beyond
    (▷ 29)
Design Within Reach
    (▷ 77)
IKEA (▷ 104)
Miss Pixie's (▷ 91)
Tabletop (▷ 91)
Woven History and Silk
    Road (▷ 66)

Malls
Fashion Centre (▷ 104)
Friendship Heights
    (▷ 104)
Gallery Place (▷ 29)
Potomac Mills Mall
    (▷ 104)
Tysons Corner (▷ 104)
Union Station (▷ 66)

Menswear
Alden (▷ 29)
American Apparel (▷ 29)
J. Press (▷ 29)
Thomas Pink (▷ 91)

Miscellaneous
Beadazzled (▷ 90)
Blue Mercury (▷ 90)
Coffee and the Works
    (▷ 90)
Crooked Beat Records
    (▷ 90)
Fahrney's Pens (▷ 29)
Grooming Lounge (▷ 29)
Groovy dc Cards & Gifts
    (▷ 66)
House of Musical
    Traditions (▷ 104)

Just Paper and Tea
    (▷ 77)
Kiehl's (▷ 77)
Paper Source (▷ 77)
Papyrus (▷ 66)
Smash Records (▷ 91)
Tourneau (▷ 104)
White House Gifts
    (▷ 29)

Womenswear
American Apparel (▷ 29)
Anthropologie (▷ 77)
Betsy Fisher (▷ 90)
Coup de Foudre (▷ 29)
Forecast (▷ 66)
Hu's Shoes (▷ 77)
Intermix (▷ 77)
Meeps Fashionette
    (▷ 91)
Nordstrom Rack (▷ 29)
Proper Topper (▷ 29, 91)
Rizik Brothers (▷ 91)
Secondi (▷ 91)
Thomas Pink (▷ 91)
Urban Chic (▷ 77)
Violet Boutique (▷ 91)

Washington by Night

The mix of illuminated white marble and hard-working youngsters looking for relief after work makes Washington a vibrant place at night. Hot spots around town are busy early and stay open late even on some weeknights, especially in the warmer months when people seek outdoor and rooftop seating.

Going Out

Young professionals tend to head to areas like U Street and Chinatown, the hot spots of the moment; Dupont Circle; Adams-Morgan, which can get overcrowded with the 20-something crowd; Capitol Hill—quick access after work; and the area around the Clarendon Metro stop in Arlington, where many Hill staffers (▷ 123) live. More mature diners and revelers tend to stick to the suburbs, especially Bethesda and Alexandria. But Washington DC feels like a town where everyone is in college—senators are even "junior" and "senior." People of all ages and interests socialize together.

Monuments in the Moonlight

If you don't feel like partying, a tour by car or on foot can be equally stimulating. The monuments and memorials, glorious in the sunlight, are entrancing in the moonlight. The Capitol looms on its hill over the Mall. The Lincoln Memorial stands guard at one end of Memorial Bridge, as does the Jefferson Memorial at the Tidal Basin. And the stark white Washington Monument is visible from most points in town.

NAVAL OBSERVATORY

On selected Mondays, the US Naval Observatory, where astronomers made measurements in preparation for the Apollo moon missions, offers a peek at the stars through its 12-inch refracting telescope. Tours start at 8.30pm and include talks on the history of the Observatory and with a member of its Time Service Department, which maintains an atomic clock. Reservations should be made 4–6 weeks in advance at www.usno.navy.mil/USNO/tours-events.

Some of the many ways to spend an evening in Washington (above)

Eating Out

Washington has long been home to dark-paneled, meat-and-potatoes places popular among older lawmakers and the lobbyists eager to ply them. But, in recent years, droves of young people have inspired restaurateurs to open good, inexpensive options as well as giving them the freedom to push the culinary envelope in an effort to sate increasingly adventurous tastes.

Top Chefs
Benefiting from lush swaths of nearby farmland, the seafood-rich Chesapeake Bay, as well as the undeniable talent of chefs like Art Smith (at Art and Soul), José Andrés (at Zaytinya, Jaleo and Oyamel), Cathal Armstrong (at Restaurant Eve) and Michel Richard (at Central) are truly taking cuisine to new levels. Their restaurants and others no longer have to be qualified as simply "good for DC;" they're objectively a treat. And this is just the beginning. As once-funky areas of Washington become more gentrified, top chefs are following. Although you can generally expect a short wait during the week, don't make the mistake of going out without reservations on Friday or Saturday nights anywhere in town.

International Cuisine
Washington DC's diverse population hailing from all countries and states has spawned a restaurant scene that spans a wide array of options at a wide range of prices. Home to the second largest population of Ethiopians outside of Ethiopia, DC dishes out more than its share of this east African cuisine, especially in Georgetown, Adams-Morgan and Shaw. Likewise, a sizeable El Salvadorian crowd has set up restaurants and *pupuserias* in Mount Pleasant and Columbia Heights. In addition, West African, Thai, Chinese, Greek, Lebanese and Indian cuisines, among countless others, put up a good fight for their fair share of restaurant space. And don't forget that there is a strong southern influence; soul food abounds.

Mouthwatering fruit salad (top); fusion food and fine cuisine (middle); alfresco dining (bottom)

Restaurants by Cuisine

There are restaurants to suit all tastes and budgets in Washington. On this page they are listed by cuisine. For a more detailed description of each restaurant, see Washington by Area.

American
Central (▷ 31)
Clyde's (▷ 31)
Equinox (▷ 31)
Founding Farmers (▷ 31)
Georgia Brown's (▷ 31)
Grapeseed (▷ 106)
Inn at Little Washington (▷ 106)
Komi (▷ 93)
Mitsitam Café (▷ 52)
The Monocle Restaurant (▷ 68)
NOPA Kitchen and Bar (▷ 32)
Nora (▷ 94)
Range (▷ 106)
Restaurant Eve (▷ 106)

Asian
Miss Saigon (▷ 80)
Muze (▷ 52)
Pho 75 (▷ 106)
Sushi Taro (▷ 94)
Teaism (▷ 94)
Thai Chef (▷ 94)

Burgers
Ben's Chili Bowl (▷ 93)
Ray's to the Third (▷ 106)
Satellite (▷ 94)

French
Bistro Bis (▷ 68)
Bistro Français (▷ 80)
Café Bonaparte (▷ 80)
Le Diplomate (▷ 93)
Montmartre (▷ 68)

Indian
Aroma Indian (▷ 31)
The Bombay Club (▷ 31)
Indique (▷ 93)

Italian
Matchbox (▷ 32)
Pizzeria Paradiso (▷ 80)
Ristorante Tosca (▷ 32)

Latin
Banana Café and Piano Bar (▷ 68)

Mediterranean
Jaleo (▷ 32)
Lebanese Taverna (▷ 94)
Mezè (▷ 94)
Veranda on P (▷ 32)
Zaytinya (▷ 32)

Mexican
Lauriol Plaza (▷ 94)
La Loma (▷ 68)
Oyamel (▷ 32)
Rosa Mexicano (▷ 32)
Well-Dressed Burrito (▷ 94)

Miscellaneous
Amsterdam Falafelshop (▷ 93)
Belga Café (▷ 68)
Brixton (▷ 93)
Bukom Café (▷ 93)
Busboys and Poets (▷ 93)

La Kazbah Marrakech (▷ 32)
Leopold's Kafe and Konditorei (▷ 80)
Nick's Riverside Grill (▷ 80)
Russia House Lounge (▷ 94)

Picnics, Soups & Sandwiches
Breadline (▷ 31)
Dean and Deluca (▷ 80)
Firehook (▷ 68)
Pavilion Café (▷ 52)

Seafood
1789 (▷ 80)
Granville Moore's (▷ 106)
Hank's Oyster Bar (▷ 93)
Market Lunch (▷ 68)

Steak
Charlie Palmer Steak (▷ 68)
Fogo de Chao Churrascaria (▷ 31)
Ray's the Steaks (▷ 106)
Social Reform Kitchen and Bar (▷ 32)

Top Tips For...

These great suggestions will help you tailor your ideal visit to Washington, no matter how you choose to spend your time. Each sight or listing has a fuller write-up elsewhere in the book.

A BIRD'S-EYE VIEW

Look over Downtown, the Capitol (▷ 60) and the Mall from the 270ft (82m) observation deck of the Old Post Office Building Tower (▷ 50).
Sip cocktails at the POV roof terrace of the W Hotel (▷ 30) with a magnificent view of the Washington Monument.
Enjoy the 360-degree panorama over the Potomac and Foggy Bottom from the John F. Kennedy Center's (▷ 74) terraces.

TRAIPSING AROUND TOWN IN FANCY SHOES

Peruse Hu's Shoes' (▷ 77) unparalleled selection of high-end women's footwear.
Don't pay a fortune for a trendy pair of shoes, instead go to Nordstrom Rack (▷ 29) for some real bargains.

The Capitol (above); Hu's Shoes (below); Willard Intercontinental Hotel (bottom)

DINING OUT OF THE BOX

Sample Austrian cuisine and mouthwatering pastries at Leopold's Kafe and Konditorei (▷ 80).
Enjoy the fresh flavors at Nora (▷ 94), America's first "organic" restaurant.

PASSING HOTSHOTS IN THE LOBBY

Sit by the fire in the Ritz-Carlton (▷ 112) but play it cool with passing ambassadors, politicos and sheiks.
Drink in the history in the ornate lobby of the Willard Intercontinental (▷ 112), a short walk from the White House.

Spa pampering (below);
classical music at the
Kennedy Center (middle)

BEING PAMPERED

Soak up the shaving lather and Musk in the plush Grooming Lounge (▷ 29).
Get the full treatment at the soothing spa in the Mandarin Oriental (▷ 112).
Enjoy the wellness-themed rooms, morning smoothies and yoga channel at Topaz Hotel (▷ 111), located in Dupont.

WATCHING WORLD-CLASS THEATER

Enjoy superbly acted and staged plays by Shakespeare and his peers at the Shakespeare Theatre (▷ 30).
Catch the world's best touring acts—from theater to music to dance—at the regal John F. Kennedy Center (▷ 74).
Go back in time and glimpse the avant garde at the home of the Woolly Mammoth Theatre Company (▷ 30), DC's Steppenwolf.

KEEPING MONEY IN YOUR POCKET

Peruse the Smithsonian's free locations, from the National Zoological Park (▷ 84) to the National Air and Space Museum (▷ 40–41) and the National Gallery of Art (▷ 43).
Explore the almost 2,000 acres (810ha) of Rock Creek Park's (▷ 86) recreational space.

Rock Creek cyclists
(above); fine wines on
offer at Washington's
bars (below)

A GREAT SELECTION AT THE BAR

Sip one of the bartenders' expert recommendations at Sonoma Wine Bar (▷ 67).
Wet your whistle with the world's best beers at Birreria Paradiso (▷ 78).
Try a pint of Belgium's finest at Belga Café (▷ 68).

KEEPING YOUR KIDS OCCUPIED

Entertaining the kids (below)

Let them play among America's flying machines at the National Air and Space Museum (▷ 40–41).

Discover the history of America's original inhabitants in the National Museum of the American Indian (▷ 44).

Wander amid the National Museum of Natural History's (▷ 50) dinosaur bones.

Let the Smithsonian Discovery Theater (▷ 49) dazzle with puppet shows, music and storytelling.

EATING WHERE LOCALS EAT

Slather your selection in beans and beef at this late-night institution: Ben's Chili Bowl (▷ 93).

Sip a frozen margarita on Lauriol Plaza's (▷ 94) roof deck amid young Hill staffers.

GETTING OUTDOORS

Follow the towpath along the Chesapeake & Ohio (C&O) Canal (▷ 75), through the forest from Georgetown to Maryland.

Wander among trees from almost every state at the National Arboretum (▷ 102).

Enjoy the verdant Bishop's Garden (▷ 88) in the shadow of the National Cathedral (▷ 87).

Ben's Chili Bowl (above middle); not just trees at the National Arboretum (above)

SHOPPING WITH THE CHIC SET

Smell the flowers, sample the cheese and sip a cappuccino at Dean and Deluca (▷ 80) amid Georgetowners shopping for gourmet treats.

Check out vintage home furnishings in the fun showroom that is Miss Pixie's (▷ 91) on the up-and-coming 14th Street.

The popular Dean and Deluca in Georgetown (right)

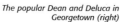

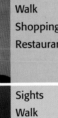

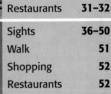

Downtown

This area, stretching from Chinatown west to the White House, has boomed in the last few years and is the city's nerve center. The district is especially popular at night.

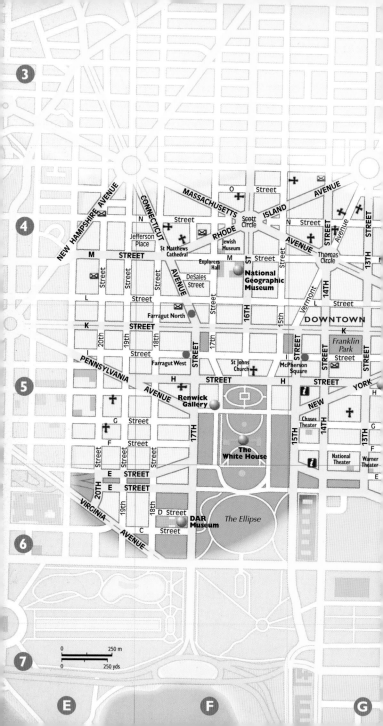

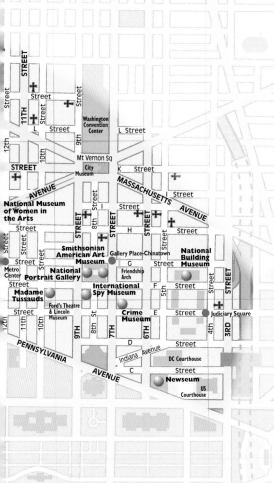

STREET

11th

12th

Street

Street

Street

Street

9th

10th

Washington
Convention
Center

L Street

STREET

Mt Vernon Sq

City
Museum

K Street

MASSACHUSETTS

AVENUE

National Museum
of Women in
the Arts

Street

Street

8th

STREET

STREET

Street

H

Street

Street

AVENUE

Smithsonian
American Art
Museum

Gallery Place–Chinatown

National
Building
Museum

Metro
Center

Street

National
Portrait Gallery

G

Street

Friendship
Arch

Street

STREET

3RD STREET

Madame
Tussauds

International
Spy Museum

F

Street

5th

Street

Judiciary Square

Ford's Theatre
& Lincoln
Museum

Crime
Museum

E

Street

4th

9TH

8th St

7TH

6TH

D

Street

11th

10th

12th

Street

Indiana Avenue

DC Courthouse

PENNSYLVANIA

AVENUE

C

Street

Newseum

US
Courthouse

Ⓗ   Ⓙ

International Spy Museum

TOP 25

The International Spy Museum illustrates the work of famous spies and explains the role of espionage

THE BASICS

www.spymuseum.org

✚ H5

✉ 800 F Street NW

☎ 202/393-7798

🕐 Times vary according to the date, so check online

💰 Expensive

♿ Excellent

Ⓜ Gallery Place–Chinatown

HIGHLIGHTS

● Interactive spy experiences
● Exquisitely Evil: 50 Years of Bond Villains

The International Spy Museum has the largest collection of espionage artifacts ever placed on public display. Plan to spend at least two hours and don't miss the entire floor dedicated to James Bond.

Spies throughout history This is the place of dreams for anyone who's ever secretly wished they could cut it as a spy. Hundreds of historic artifacts, photographs, films and videos recall the most famous espionage events in history— from the Greek and Roman empires to the British Empire, both World Wars and, of course, the Cold War. Visitors receive a "cover identity" when they enter and learn about the tradecraft and tools of spying through the ages, watch films about real spies, and find out about the challenges facing current-day spies.

Role playing The immersive interactive exhibit, Operation Spy, lets visitors play spy for an hour and try to complete a mission to intercept a secret weapons deal involving a nuclear device. The interactive exhibit, Exquisitely Evil: 50 Years of Bond Villains, celebrates the Golden Anniversary (2012) of the film franchise of the most famous spy of all times, James Bond. The exhibit focuses on Bond's best-known adversaries, from Dr. No to Auric Goldfinger, and looks at how the films were inspired by the threats the world was facing when they were made. For an extra charge you can take part in a spy game the museum runs in Downtown DC.

The White House

1600 Pennsylvania Avenue, the White House, first occupied by John Adams in 1800

THE BASICS

www.nps.gov/whho

➕ F5

✉ 1600 Pennsylvania Avenue

☎ 202/456-7041

🕐 Tue–Thu 7.30am–11.30am, Fri, Sat 7.30–1.30

💲 Free

♿ Excellent

Ⓜ McPherson Square, Metro Center

❓ You are usually required to write to a Member of Congress up to six months in advance to be accepted on a free tour. Foreign visitors should contact their embassy in Washington. For historical exhibits, go to the White House Visitor Center, 1450 Pennsylvania Avenue NW 🕐 Daily 7.30–4 Ⓜ Federal Triangle, Metro Center

In the city's oldest public building, virtually every desk, every sterling tea service, every silver platter, decanter, painting and floor has witnessed historic events of the American democracy.

The "President's Palace" When he became the second occupant in 1801 of what was then known as the "President's Palace," Thomas Jefferson (1743–1826) thought James Hoban's (c.1762–1831) original design "big enough for two emperors, one Pope and the grand Lama." Since then the building has had several renovations. The first was necessary after the British burned it in 1814. An almost-complete renovation occurred during the Truman Administration (1945–53) after a piano broke through the floor, and an engineer determined that the building was staying erect only out of "force of habit."

Works of art The president's house holds an impressive display of decorative arts from the Sheraton, French and American Empire, Queen Anne and Federal periods. There are carved Carrara marble mantels, Bohemian cut-glass chandeliers and Turkish Hereke carpets. The tour may vary depending on official functions, but usually open are the ceremonial East Room, with Gilbert Stuart's 1797 *George Washington* portrait, the Vermeil Room containing 17th- and early 18th-century French and English gilded silver (vermeil), the small drawing room, and the neoclassical State Dining Room where George P. A. Healy's (1813–94) *Abraham Lincoln* portrait hangs.

HIGHLIGHTS

● *Abraham Lincoln*, George P. A. Healy
● China Room
● French and English gilded silver
● East Room
● *George Washington*, Gilbert Stuart

More to See

CRIME MUSEUM

www.crimemuseum.org

Here you will find five galleries dedicated to forensic science and crime scene investigation.

🔲 H6 ✉ 575 7th Street NW ☎ 202/393–1099 🕓 Mid-Mar to mid-Aug Mon–Thu 9–7, Fri, Sat 9–8, Sun 10–7; mid-Aug to mid-Mar Sun–Thu 10–7, Fri–Sat 10–8 🚇 Gallery Place–Chinatown 💷 Expensive

DAR MUSEUM

www.dar.org/museum

The National Society of the Daughters of the American Revolution has been collecting pre-Civil War, American artifacts for more than 100 years.

🔲 F6 ✉ 1776 D Street NW ☎ 202/628–1776 🕓 Mon–Fri 8.30–4, Sat 9–5 🚇 Farragut West, Farragut North 💷 Free

MADAME TUSSAUDS

www.madametussauds.com/washington

Take a tour through the glitterati of the world of politics, stage, screen and sport. Be interviewed in the Media Room and go behind the scenes to learn how the wax models are created.

🔲 G5 ✉ 1001 F Street NW ☎ 202/942–7300 🕓 Daily (but times vary so check website) 🚇 Metro Center 💷 Expensive

NATIONAL BUILDING MUSEUM

www.nbm.org

The dramatic interior of this building houses exhibits on DC's cityscape, urban planning and general architecture.

🔲 H5 ✉ 401 F Street NW ☎ 202/272–2448 🕓 Mon–Sat 10–5, Sun 11–5 🚇 Judiciary Square 💷 Moderate

NATIONAL GEOGRAPHIC MUSEUM

www.nationalgeographic.com

Best known for producing the *National Geographic Magazine*, the Society also breathes life into splendid exhibits at its headquarters by highlighting the work of its many talented photographers.

🔲 F4 ✉ 1145 17th Street NW ☎ 202/857–7700 🕓 Daily 10–6 🚇 Farragut West, Farragut North 💷 Expensive

Madame Tussauds wax museum

NATIONAL MUSEUM OF WOMEN IN THE ARTS

www.nmwa.org

The only museum in the US dedicated to the artwork of women, the collection includes around 4,500 objects by 1,000 artists from around the world from the Renaissance to the present day.

✚ G5 ✉ 1250 New York Avenue NW ☎ 202/783–5000 🕐 Mon–Sat 10–5, Sun 12–5 🚇 Metro Center ♿ Expensive

NATIONAL PORTRAIT GALLERY

www.npg.si.edu

This renovated neoclassical gallery has portraits of famous Americans crafted by other famous Americans using visual and performing arts and new media.

✚ H5 ✉ 8th and F streets NW ☎ 202/633–8300 🕐 Daily 11.30–7 🚇 Gallery Place–Chinatown ♿ Free

NEWSEUM

www.newseum.org

This monument to the First Amendment, with 14 state-of-the-art galleries, has an interactive newsroom and new media gallery.

✚ H6 ✉ 555 Pennsylvania Avenue and 6th Street NW ☎ 202/292–6100 🕐 Daily 9–5 🚇 Archives–Navy Memorial–Judiciary Square ♿ Expensive

RENWICK GALLERY

www.americanart.si.edu/renwick

Dedicated to American craft and decorative arts, the first floor hosts exceptional temporary exhibits. Closed until the end of 2015.

✚ F5 ✉ 17th Street NW and Pennsylvania Avenue ☎ 202/633–7970 🕐 Daily 11.30–7 🚇 Gallery Place–Chinatown ♿ Free

SMITHSONIAN AMERICAN ART MUSEUM

www.americanart.si.edu

America's first national art collection includes works by Georgia O'Keeffe, Edward Hopper and Roy Lichtenstein, in the same building as the National Portrait Gallery.

✚ H5 ✉ 8th and F streets NW ☎ 202/633–7970 🕐 Daily 11.30–7 🚇 Gallery Place–Chinatown ♿ Free

DOWNTOWN MORE TO SEE

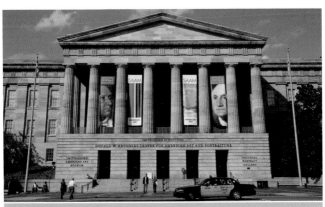

The National Portrait Gallery and Smithsonian American Art Museum

Presidential Route

A tour that passes many of the sites on the inaugural walk, finishing at the White House.

DISTANCE: 2.25 miles (3.6km) **ALLOW:** 2 hours 45 minutes

START

US CAPITOL (▷ 60–61)
✚ J6 🚇 Union Station, Capitol South

❶ Begin on the west steps of the Capitol building (▷ 60–61). The view takes in Washington's famous museums and monuments, from the US Botanic Garden (▷ 58–59) and federal office buildings (left along Maryland Avenue), to the Washington Monument (▷ 46–47) and Lincoln Memorial (▷ 38) directly ahead, to the domes of the National Museum of Natural History (▷ 50) and the National Gallery of Art (▷ 43), on the right.

❷ Follow Pennsylvania Avenue past I. M. Pei's East Building of the National Gallery of Art and on past the Newseum to the National Archives (▷ 42) and Navy Memorial.

❸ Turn right onto 7th Street and follow it up through DC's quickly gentrifying Chinatown to the National Portrait Gallery (▷ 27).

END

THE WHITE HOUSE (▷ 25)
✚ F5 🚇 McPherson Square, Metro Center

❼ Take a left onto Pennsylvania Avenue, passing between Lafayette Park and the White House (▷ 25).

❻ Turn right onto 15th Street, past the 1836 Treasury Building, which you might recognize from a $10 bill.

❺ Continue south on 10th Street and then turn right onto Pennsylvania Avenue. The clock tower of the Old Post Office (▷ 50) across the intersection offers views of the city. Farther up Pennsylvania you will pass Freedom Plaza, with its stone map of L'Enfant's city plan, and Pershing Park.

❹ Head west along G Street and then turn left on 10th Street. Two blocks south you will pass Ford's Theatre (▷ 30), where Abraham Lincoln was fatally wounded in 1865. The FBI Building is across E Street on the left.

Shopping

ALDEN
www.aldenshoe.com
Alden, originally of New England, sells good quality men's shoes and boots as well as leather accessories.
⊞ H5 ⊠ 921 F Street NW ☎ 202/347-2308 ⏰ Mon–Fri 10–6, Sat 11–5 Ⓜ Metro Center

AMERICAN APPAREL
www.americanapparel.net
This temple to the T-shirt and other simple cotton clothing draws a congregation of DC hipsters.
⊞ G5 ⊠ 1090 F Street NW ☎ 202/628-0438 ⏰ Mon–Sat 11–9, Sun 12–8 Ⓜ Metro Center

BED BATH & BEYOND
This mega home store has everything from bedding and candles to kitchenware.
⊞ H5 ⊠ 709 7th Street NW ☎ 202/628-0002 ⏰ Mon–Sat 9.30–9.30, Sun 10–6 Ⓜ Gallery Place–Chinatown

COUP DE FOUDRE
www.coupdefoudrelingerie.com
"Love at First Sight" carries high-end European lingerie in its elegant boudoir.
⊞ G6 ⊠ Corner of 11th and E Street NW ☎ 202/393-0878 ⏰ Mon–Sat 11–6 Ⓜ Metro Center

FAHRNEY'S PENS
www.fahrneyspens.com
This DC institution stocks traditional and cutting-edge pens and stationery.
⊞ G5 ⊠ 1317 F Street NW ☎ 202/628-9525 ⏰ Mon–Fri 9.30–6, Sat 10–5 Ⓜ Metro Center

GALLERY PLACE
www.galleryplace.com
Gallery Place complex has a movie theater, a bowling alley and retailers like Urban Outfitters.
⊞ H5 ⊠ 7th and H streets NW ⏰ Hours vary Ⓜ Gallery Place–Chinatown

GROOMING LOUNGE
www.groominglounge.com
The Lounge pampers the modern male with fine grooming and shaving products, shoe shines, shaves and haircuts.
⊞ F4 ⊠ 1745 L Street NW ☎ 202/466-8900 ⏰ Mon–Fri 9–7, Sat 9–6, Sun 10–5.15 Ⓜ Farragut North, Farragut West

J. PRESS
www.jpressonline.com
This traditional clothier still strives to "dress men to the Ivy League standard."
⊞ F4 ⊠ 1801 L Street NW ☎ 202/857-0120 ⏰ Mon–Fri 9–6.30, Sat

BASIC NEEDS
Radio Shack sells voltage converters (732 7th Street NW and other locations, 202/638-5689; www.radioshack.com). For shoe repairs, try Cleveland Park Valet (3303 Connecticut Ave NW; www.clevelandpark.com/cpvalet). Also try the DC Visitor Information Center (▷ 123).

9.30–6 Ⓜ Farragut North, Farragut West

NORDSTROM RACK
This popular discount clothing and shoe chain offers high-quality items from Nordstrom's department store at a fraction of the price.
⊞ E4 ⊠ 18th and L streets NW ☎ 202/627-3650 ⏰ Mon–Fri 9–8, Sat 10–8, Sun 12–6 Ⓜ Farragut West

PROPER TOPPER
www.propertopper.com
In addition to great hats, charming accessories and home furnishings, you'll find unique women's and children's wear.
⊞ F4 ⊠ 1350 Connecticut Ave NW ☎ 202/842-3055 ⏰ Mon–Fri 10–8, Sat 10–7, Sun 12–6 Ⓜ Dupont Circle

REITER'S BOOKS
Washington's oldest independent bookstore features scientific, technical and professional titles, plus puzzles, games and toys for children of all ages.
⊞ E4–5 ⊠ 1900 G Street NW ☎ 202/223-3327 ⏰ Mon–Fri 9.30–6 Sat 10–5 Ⓜ Farragut West

WHITE HOUSE GIFTS
www.whitehousegifts.com
Situated directly opposite the White House, this showcases political memorabilia and souvenirs.
⊞ G5 ⊠ 701 15th Street NW ☎ 202/737-9500 ⏰ Mon–Sat 8am–9pm, Sun 9–8 Ⓜ Metro Center

DOWNTOWN SHOPPING

Entertainment and Nightlife

DAR CONSTITUTION HALL

www.dar.org/constitution-hall
This 3,700-seat hall hosts music, stage shows and comedy acts.
✚ F6 ✉ 18th and C streets NW ☎ 202/628-1776
Ⓜ Farragut West, then walk six blocks south

FORD'S THEATRE

www.fordstheatre.org
Hosts mainly musicals, many with family appeal.
✚ G5 ✉ 511 10th Street NW ☎ 202/347-4833
Ⓜ Metro Center

NATIONAL THEATRE

www.thenationaldc.org
Presents pre- and post-Broadway shows.
✚ G6 ✉ 1321 Pennsylvania Avenue NW ☎ 202/628-6161 Ⓜ Metro Center

POSTE

www.postebrasserie.com
Poste's huge courtyard patio at the Hotel Monaco mixes well with the bartender's tasty seasonal alcohol infusions.
✚ H5 ✉ 555 8th Street NW ☎ 202/783-6060
🕐 Bar hours: daily from 10.30am (closing times vary)
Ⓜ Gallery Place–Chinatown

POV ROOF TERRACE

www.wwashingtondc.com/pov
Take in stunning views while indulging in superb cocktails and light bites.
✚ G5 ✉ 515 15th Street NW ☎ 202/661-2400
🕐 From 3pm Mon–Fri and 11am Sat–Sun. Check website
Ⓜ McPherson Square

RFD

www.lovethebeer.com
RFD is frequently packed, with a lively atmosphere and huge beer list.
✚ H5 ✉ 810 7th Street NW ☎ 202/289-2030
🕐 Mon–Thu 11am–2am, Fri–Sat 11am–3am, Sun 11am–midnight Ⓜ Gallery Place–Chinatown

ROUND ROBIN BAR

www.washington.intercontinental.com
This circular, mahogany bar maintains the same atmosphere it did in the early 19th century when Senator Henry Clay introduced the bartender, and DC, to the mint julep.
✚ G6 ✉ 1401 Pennsylvania Avenue NW ☎ 202/628-9100
🕐 Mon–Sat noon–1am, Sun 12–12 Ⓜ Metro Center

SCIENCE CLUB

www.scienceclubdc.com
A narrow, multistory lounge with chic decor, a veg-friendly menu and DJs in the back room.

WHERE THE ACTION IS

Screen on the Green
On Monday nights throughout July and August the Mall is turned into a free open-air cinema screening classic films, from Elvis Presley musicals to Hitchcock's thrillers. Washingtonians arrive as early as 5pm to save a spot and picnic on the lawn stretching between 7th and 12th streets.

✚ E4 ✉ 1136 19th Street NW ☎ 202/775-0747
🕐 Mon–Thu 5pm–2am, Fri–Sat 5pm–3am Ⓜ Farragut North

SHAKESPEARE THEATRE

www.shakespearetheatre.org
This theater offers fantastically staged and acted performances of works by the Bard and his contemporaries.
✚ H6 ✉ 450 7th Street NW (Lansburgh Theatre), 610 F Street NW (Sidney Harman Hall) ☎ 202/547-1122
Ⓜ Gallery Place–Chinatown

LA TASCA

www.latascausa.com
Spanish tapas, sangria-soaked happy hours and flamenco performances.
✚ H5 ✉ 722 7th Street NW ☎ 202/347-9190 🕐 Sun–Thu 11–10, Fri, Sat 11–11
Ⓜ Gallery Place–Chinatown

VERIZON CENTER

www.verizoncenter.com
The 20,000-seat home of Washington's pro basketball and hockey teams also hosts DC's biggest concerts and the circus.
✚ H5 ✉ 601 F Street NW ☎ 202/628-3200 Ⓜ Gallery Place–Chinatown

WOOLLY MAMMOTH THEATRE COMPANY

www.woollymammoth.net
This resident group presents unusual, avant-garde shows in its modern space.
✚ H6 ✉ 641 D Street NW ☎ 202/393-3939 Ⓜ Gallery Place–Chinatown

Restaurants

AROMA INDIAN ($$)

www.aromarestaurant.com
This is a favorite of employees from the nearby World Bank and International Monetary Fund. There's a huge menu and popular lunch specials.
🔲 E5 ✉ 1919 I Street NW ☎ 202-833-4700 🕐 Mon–Sat 11.30–2.30, 5.30–10 🚇 Farragut West

THE BOMBAY CLUB ($$–$$$)

www.bombayclubdc.com
A block from the White House, this beautiful Indian restaurant emulates a private British club in 19th-century India.
🔲 F5 ✉ 815 Connecticut Avenue NW ☎ 202/659–3727 🕐 Mon–Fri lunch, dinner; Sat dinner; Sun 5.30–9.30 🚇 Farragut North

BREADLINE ($)

www.breadline.com
This one-of-a-kind bakery-café, a favorite among White House staff, turns out warm rolls, a variety of sandwiches and home-made soups.
🔲 F5 ✉ 1751 Pennsylvania Avenue NW ☎ 202/822–8900 🕐 Mon–Fri 7–5.30 🚇 Farragut West

CENTRAL ($$$)

www.centralmichelrichard.com
Michel Richard's award-winning bistro serves American cuisine with a French twist. Very popular so reserve ahead.
🔲 G6 ✉ 1001 Pennsylvania Avenue NW ☎ 202/626–0015 🕐 Sun–Fri lunch, Mon–Sat dinner 🚇 Metro Center

CLYDE'S ($$)

www.clydes.com/gallery-place
There's something for everyone on the vast American-fare menu in this soaring, grand saloon and restaurant.
🔲 H5 ✉ 707 7th Street NW ☎ 202/349–3700 🕐 Mon–Thu 11am–2am, Fri 11am–3am, Sat 10am–3am, Sun 10am–2am 🚇 Gallery Place–Chinatown

EQUINOX ($$$)

www.equinoxrestaurant.com
Chef Todd Gray uses seasonal ingredients to build beautiful and traditional regional dishes, including Chesapeake oysters and bacon-wrapped Cervena venison. Try the chef's 5-course tasting menu. Reservations requested.
🔲 F5 ✉ 818 Connecticut Avenue NW ☎ 202/331–8118 🕐 Mon–Fri lunch; daily dinner 🚇 Farragut West

FOGO DE CHAO CHURRASCARIA ($$$)

www.fogodechao.com
For a flat price at this authentic Brazilian steakhouse, diners get their choice of unlimited, succulent roasted meat and fish, plus the massive salad and vegetable bar.
🔲 G6 ✉ 1101 Pennsylvania Ave NW ☎ 202/347–4668 🕐 Mon–Fri lunch; dinner all week 🚇 Federal Triangle

FOUNDING FARMERS ($$)

www.wearefoundingfarmers.com
This restaurant serves seasonal food from farms local and not so local.
🔲 F5 ✉ 1924 Pennsylvania Avenue NW ☎ 202/822–8783 🕐 Mon–Fri breakfast, lunch, Sat–Sun brunch, daily dinner 🚇 Farragut West–Foggy Bottom

GEORGIA BROWN'S ($$$)

www.gbrowns.com
This elegant restaurant attracts government

officials and journalists with its southern specials.

F5 950 15th Street NW
202/393–4499 Mon–Sat lunch, dinner; Sun brunch, dinner McPherson Square

JALEO ($$)

www.jaleo.com

A lively tapas restaurant, José Andrés' Jaleo serves up small plates that cater to any craving, whether it be for homemade chorizo or fried squid with aioli.

H6 480 7th Street NW
202/628–7949 Daily lunch, dinner Gallery Place–Chinatown

LA KAZBAH MARRAKECH ($$)

www.lakazbah.com

Beautifully decorated Moroccan/Mediterranean restaurant with daily lunch specials, belly dancing and upstairs hookah bar.

E4 2147 P Street NW
202/775–1882 Daily 11.30–11 Dupont Circle

MATCHBOX ($$)

www.matchboxchinatown.com

This warm, stylish pizzeria impresses with wood-oven, gourmet pies and miniburgers, plus a pleasant deck with a fireplace.

H5 713 H Street NW
202/289–4441 Daily lunch, dinner Gallery Place–Chinatown

NOPA KITCHEN AND BAR ($$)

www.nopadc.com

Elegant, 160-seat brasserie serving American fare

with French and Asian influences.

H5 800 F Street NW
202/347–4667 Sun–Fri lunch; dinner daily Gallery Place–Chinatown

OYAMEL ($$$)

www.oyamel.com

Another of José Andrés' ventures, serving some of the best cocktails in town, solid Oaxacan cuisine and a live, projected view of a Mexican market.

H6 401 7th Street NW
202/628–1005 Daily lunch, dinner Archives

RISTORANTE TOSCA ($$$)

www.toscadc.com

Northern Italian dishes are cooked to perfection in this comfortable, beige dining room.

G5 1112 F Street NW
202/367–1990 Mon–Fri lunch, Mon–Sat dinner Metro Center

RESTAURANT WEEK

For a full week each January and August, a host of Washington DC's restaurants, including some of its finest, offer three-course, fixed-price lunch menus for around $20 and dinner menus for around $35. Some restaurants only offer a limited selection and others only offer lunch or dinner, not both. Make reservations well in advance.
www.ramw.org/restaurantweek

ROSA MEXICANO ($$)

www.rosamexicano.com

Rosa Mexicano specializes in pomegranate margaritas and high-end Mexican food.

H5 575 7th Street NW
202/783–5522 Daily lunch, dinner Gallery Place–Chinatown

SOCIAL REFORM KITCHEN AND BAR ($$–$$$)

www.socialreformbar.com

This clubby steak parlor is where the powerful talk politics over rib-eyes and creamed spinach.

H6 401 9th Street NW
202/393–1300 Mon–Fri lunch; Mon–Sat dinner Archives–Navy Memorial

VERANDA ON P ($–$$)

www.verandaonp.com

Greek and Italian fare—the stuffed vine leaves are not to be missed.

G4 1100 P Street NW
202/234–6870 Mon–Thu 5pm–12.30am, Fri–Sat 5pm–1.30am, Sun 5pm–midnight, Sat–Sun brunch 10.30–3 Shaw–Howard University

ZAYTINYA ($$)

www.zaytinya.com

This Mediterranean *meze* spot is popular for its creative cocktails and inventive Turkish, Greek and Lebanese cuisine.

H5 701 9th Street NW
202/638–0800 Daily lunch, dinner Gallery Place–Chinatown

Explore the mile-long stretch of grass from the Capitol to the Washington Monument.

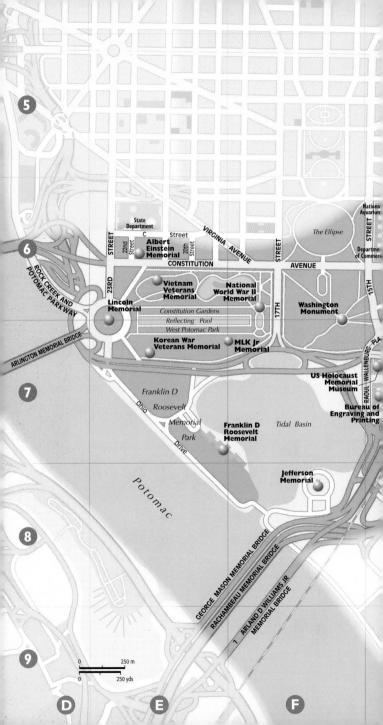

5

6

7

8

9

State
Department

C Street

Albert Einstein
Memorial

22nd Street

20th Street

STREET

23RD STREET

STREET

VIRGINIA AVENUE

CONSTITUTION AVENUE

Vietnam
Veterans
Memorial

National
World War II
Memorial

17TH STREET

15TH STREET

RAOUL WALLENBURG PLA

The Ellipse

Nationa
Aquarium

Departme
of Comme

Lincoln
Memorial

Constitution Gardens
Reflecting Pool
West Potomac Park

Korean War
Veterans Memorial

MLK Jr
Memorial

Washington
Monument

US Holocaust
Memorial
Museum

Bureau of
Engraving and
Printing

ROCK CREEK AND POTOMAC PARKWAY

ARLINGTON MEMORIAL BRIDGE

Franklin D

Roosevelt

Ohio

Memorial

Drive

Franklin D
Roosevelt
Memorial

Tidal Basin

Jefferson
Memorial

Potomac

GEORGE MASON MEMORIAL BRIDGE

RACHAMBEAU MEMORIAL BRIDGE

1 ARLAND D WILLIAMS JR
MEMORIAL BRIDGE

0   250 m

0   250 yds

D   **E**   **F**

Federal Triangle
Old Post Office

National Museum of American History

National Museum of Natural History

PENNSYLVANIA AVENUE

D St

STREET

National Archives

CONSTITUTION

Archives-Navy Memorial-Penn Quarter

AVENUE

National Gallery of Art

National Gallery of Art East Building

9TH

National Gallery of Art Sculpture Garden

Madison

The

Jefferson
Smithsonian

Smithsonian Institution

Discovery Theater

Drive

Mall

Drive

Street

3RD

4th

Avenue

National Air and Space Museum

INDEPENDENCE

Freer and Arthur M Sackler Galleries

Hirshhorn Museum and Sculpture Garden

AVENUE

Maryland

National Museum of the American Indian

C Street

13th St.

D Street

12TH

STREET

14th Street

9TH

ST

D Street

STREET

7TH

Virginia

Street

C Street

4th

Avenue

Street

STREET

US Postal Service HQ

L'Enfant Plaza

Avenue

School St

E Street

SOUTHWEST FREEWAY 395

MAINE AVENUE

Water Street

FRANCIS CASE MEMORIAL BRIDGE

Yacht Club

Washington Channel

G   H   J

FDR and Jefferson Memorials

TOP **25**

Bronze statue of Thomas Jefferson (left); the Tidal Basin (right)

THE BASICS

Jefferson Memorial
www.nps.gov/thje
➕ F8
✉ West Potomac Park, Tidal Basin, south bank
☎ 202/426–6841
🕐 Daily 24 hours. Rangers available to answer questions daily 9.30am–11.30pm 💲 Free
♿ Excellent
Ⓜ Smithsonian, then 15-min walk

FDR Memorial
www.nps.gov/frde
➕ E7
✉ West Potomac Park, Tidal Basin, west bank
☎ 202/426–6841
🕐 As for Jefferson above
💲 Free Ⓜ Smithsonian, then 10- to 15-min walk

HIGHLIGHTS

● Jefferson bronze
● Inscribed Declaration of Independence
● Wheelchair statue of FDR
● Surrounding cherry trees
● Boat rides in the Tidal Basin

The Jefferson Memorial was dedicated by President Franklin Delano Roosevelt on the 200th anniversary of Jefferson's birth, April 13, 1943. Roosevelt's own memorial was created nearby and dedicated in 1997.

Classical The contributions of Thomas Jefferson, a brilliant statesman and America's third president, are commemorated in a white-marble, neoclassical memorial along Washington's Tidal Basin amid 3,700 Japanese cherry trees. The Memorial was modeled by architect John Russell Pope (1874–1937) on buildings that Jefferson had designed himself at his own home and the University of Virginia, which, in turn, showed deference to the Pantheon in Rome. The open interior of the building has a 19ft (5.8m) bronze of Jefferson, circled by excerpts of his speeches and writings inscribed into the walls. An inscription above Jefferson reads, "I have sworn upon the altar of God eternal hostility against every form of tyranny over the mind of man."

Sculpture Franklin Delano Roosevelt (1882–1945), America's president from the Great Depression through the end of World War II, is memorialized by a park on the west side of the Tidal Basin. The Memorial, cloaked in shady trees amid waterfalls and pools, is divided into four outdoor "rooms," each commemorating one of FDR's four terms in office. Nine sets of bronze sculptures, one of which is a depiction of FDR in a wheelchair, punctuate the park.

The central fountain in the impressive courtyard at the Freer Gallery

Freer and Arthur M. Sackler Galleries

THE BASICS

www.asia.si.edu

G7

12th Street and Independence Avenue SW (galleries next door to each other)

202/633–4880

Daily 10–5.30

Free

Excellent

Smithsonian

The Freer is closed from January 2016 to the summer of 2017, but the Sackler remains open

Among the lesser known treasures of the city, the Freer and Sackler galleries contain more than 40,000 works of Asian art, as well as one of the world's largest collections of paintings by James McNeill Whistler (1834–1903).

Freer Gallery of Art Housed in a granite palazzo-style building, designed by Charles A. Platt (1861–1933), the Freer houses a wide range of art including Asian porcelains, Japanese screens, Chinese painting and bronzes, Korean stoneware and Islamic art. The Peacock Room, painted in blue and gold designs by Whistler, was once part of a London town house. The owner was away when Whistler used his fine leather walls as a canvas, and sparked an ongoing feud between the two. Freer Gallery founder, Charles Lang Freer (1854–1919), bought the room, which was installed in his Detroit home before being moved here after his death.

Arthur M. Sackler Gallery A beautifully constructed, subterranean museum, the Sackler has its own impressive collection of Asian art, including ceramics, printing, metalwork, bronzes and jades. More than 1,000 of these works were donated in 1987 by Arthur M. Sackler, a physician and publisher who subsequently gave $4 million for the construction of the building. Fantastic touring exhibits have brought portraits, Southeast Asian ceramics and Persian calligraphy to the Sackler. The Meyer Auditorium hosts Asian films, lectures, music and theater.

HIGHLIGHTS

The Freer Gallery of Art
● *The Peacock Room*, James McNeill Whistler
● *Princess from the Land of Porcelain*, James McNeill Whistler
● Ancient Chinese artifacts
● Korean ceramics
● Japanese painted screens

The Arthur M. Sackler Gallery
● Chinese jades and bronzes
● Islamic manuscripts
● Ancient Iranian metalworks

Lincoln Memorial

The Lincoln Memorial (left); sculpture of Lincoln (middle); Washington Monument (right)

THE BASICS

www.nps.gov/linc
E6
23rd Street NW between Constitution and Independence avenues (west end of the Mall)
202/426–6841
As for Jefferson Memorial (▷ 36)
Free
Excellent
Foggy Bottom–GWU

HIGHLIGHTS

● Daniel Chester French's *Lincoln*
● Inscriptions of Lincoln's 1863 Gettysburg Address and Second Inaugural Address
● Reflecting Pool
● View at sunset

So powerful and somber is this memorial that you could easily imagine Lincoln rising up and resuming his epic struggles. The view from the steps at sunset is one of the city's most romantic, with the Washington Monument reflected in the rectangular pool at its base.

Tribute Architect Henry Bacon (1866–1924) chose a Greek Doric style for Lincoln's memorial because he felt that a memorial to a man who had sacrificed so much to defend democracy should be modeled after the style found in the birthplace of democracy. Construction, during World War I, was not without difficulties. The site, a swamp, required the builders to dig down almost 65ft (19.8m) to find a suitable foundation. Almost 38,000 tons of material was transported from locations as far away as Colorado.

History in stone Bacon's white marble temple to Lincoln contains Daniel Chester French's (1850–1931) 19ft (5.8m) seated statue of the president. The statue was so large that it had to be constructed inside the memorial. Its chamber is flanked by two smaller rooms, which contain inscriptions of Lincoln's Gettysburg and second inaugural addresses and two beautiful murals. The area surrounding the Reflecting Pool that stretches east from the foot of the monument has hosted seminal events in America's history, most notably Martin Luther King, Jr.'s "I Have a Dream" speech.

The impressive statue of Martin Luther King, Jr. stands 29.5ft (9m) high and is the centerpiece of the memorial

Martin Luther King, Jr. Memorial

Visitors to the Dr. Martin Luther King, Jr. Memorial take the same symbolic journey that the famous civil rights leader took—they pass through a boulder that has been split in two and named "Mountain of Despair" and emerge at the "Stone of Hope," a reference to his famous speech.

Years of planning It took more than two decades of planning and fundraising to establish this memorial to the famous American civil rights leader, Martin Luther King, Jr. (1929–68), who followed in the nonviolent footsteps of Mahatma Gandhi. The address on the white granite memorial, which was dedicated on October 16, 2011, is 1964 Independence Avenue SW, in commemoration of the year the Civil Rights Act of 1964 became law.

A symbolic struggle The key message, and symbol, of the memorial is a line from King's "I Have a Dream" speech, which he delivered on the steps of the Lincoln Memorial in 1963: "Out of a mountain of despair, a stone of hope." The memorial's president, Harry E. Johnson, said the 4-acre (1.6ha) site was "envisioned as a quiet and peaceful space, yet drawing from Dr. King's speeches and using his own rich language, the King Memorial will almost certainly change the heart of every person who visits…a public sanctuary where future generations of Americans, regardless of race, religion, gender, ethnicity or sexual orientation, can come to honor Dr. King."

THE BASICS

www.nps.gov/mlkm

🚻 E7

✉ 1964 Independence Avenue SW

☎ 202/426–6841

🕐 As for Jefferson Memorial (▷ 36)

💷 Free

♿ Excellent

🚇 Smithsonian, then a 10- to 15-min walk

❓ The memorial is located at the northwest corner of the Tidal Basin near the Franklin Delano Roosevelt Memorial

HIGHLIGHTS

● The Mountain of Despair
● The Stone of Hope
● Inscription wall with famous speech passages
● 29.5ft (9m) high stone relief of Dr. King

National Air and Space Museum

HIGHLIGHTS

- Wright brothers' *Flyer*
- Charles Lindbergh's *Spirit of St. Louis*
- Chuck Yeager's *Bell X-1 Glamorous Glennis*
- The Steven F. Udvar-Hazy Center
- John Glenn's *Friendship* and *Apollo 11*
- *Discovery* Space Shuttle
- Skylab Command Module
- Lunar exploration vehicles

TIP

- Looking for smaller crowds? Head out to the hangars at the Udvar-Hazy Center, where you can also see an array of impressive flying machines.

The most visited museum on the Mall takes adults and children alike on a pioneering journey from the first manned motorized flight to the most recent space exploration—"infinity and beyond!"

Flight pioneers The Smithsonian's bicentennial gift to the nation, this museum receives almost 9 million visitors a year in its monumental glass-and-granite galleries. The collection—begun as early as 1861, when the first secretary of the Smithsonian urged experiments in balloon flight—includes the Wright brothers' 1903 *Flyer*, Charles Lindbergh's *Spirit of St. Louis*, Chuck Yeager's *Bell X-1*, in which he broke the sound barrier, and *The Voyager*, the plane in which Dick Rutan and Jeana Yeager flew nonstop around the world in 1986.

The Apollo lunar rover (left) and space rockets (right) at the National Air and Space Musuem

Into space Visitors can touch a moon rock and see the *Apollo 11* and Skylab command modules, and the *Discovery* Space Shuttle. Aside from the *Milestones of Flight*, which is being renovated, this museum also houses exhibits on the half-century space race between the United States and the Soviet Union, exploring the planets of our solar system, the global positioning system and the science of flight, among many others. Visitors who tire of the museum's colossal collection can take in an IMAX film, go for a test run in a flight simulator, or visit the Albert Einstein Planetarium and discover the universe on the *Journey to the Stars*. Despite its huge size, this building can only hold about 10 percent of the Museum's collection. Most of the rest is housed in hangars at the Steven F. Udvar-Hazy Center near Dulles International Airport.

THE BASICS

www.airandspace.si.edu

✚ H7

✉ Independence Avenue at 6th Street SW

☎ 202/633–2214

🕐 Daily 10–5.30

💷 Free. Albert Einstein Planetarium: moderate

♿ Excellent

🍴 Wright Place Food Court

🚇 L'Enfant Plaza, Smithsonian

❓ Lockheed Martin IMAX, Udvar-Hazy IMAX: call for schedules. Tours daily

National Archives

The National Archives (left); inspecting the Archives' historic documents (right)

THE BASICS

www.archives.gov

⊞ H6

✉ Constitution Avenue at 7th Street NW

☎ 877/444–6777

🕐 Daily 10–5.30

💵 Free

♿ Excellent

🚇 Archives–Navy Memorial

❓ Guided tours Mon–Fri 9.45am (reservations required)

HIGHLIGHTS

● Charters of Freedom
● Murals by Barry Faulkner
● Changing exhibition gallery

Behind this building's colossal bronze doors, America's story comes alive through millions of primary materials, including the founding documents, the rifle used to shoot John F. Kennedy (1917–63) and the Watergate tapes.

Charters of Freedom Under low light in the magnificent central rotunda lie 14 of America's founding documents, including the Constitution, the Declaration of Independence and the Bill of Rights. All have been encased in state-of-the-art, gold-plated, titanium frames filled with inert argon gas. Two 340lb (154.5kg) murals, *The Constitution* and *The Declaration of Independence*, accentuate the experience.

Archival splendor The Archives is most famous for the Charters of Freedom, but this building contains billions of other documents, maps and photographs, plus hundreds of thousands of miles of film and videotapes, the most entertaining and instructional of which are on display in the Public Vaults. This child-friendly area showcases audio recordings of congressional debates on prohibition, video clips of former Presidents cracking jokes and behind-the-scenes conversations between President Kennedy and his advisors during the Cuban Missile Crisis, among many other exhibits, all displayed in accessible multimedia presentations. The William G. McGowan Theater screens films about the Archives and the Charters of Freedom by day and documentary films at night.

National Gallery of Art

Monet's *Woman with a Parasol (left); the dome of the main atrium (right)*

The two buildings of the Gallery, filled with serene spots to sit and reflect, are reason enough to visit, but they also house one of the world's most incredible art collections ranging from the Middle Ages to the modern day.

West Building Designed by John Russell Pope in the classical style, this building was funded by a gift from Andrew Mellon, a former treasury secretary. Mellon also donated an impressive collection of art that has been augmented to fill the building's many galleries. Of particular interest are da Vinci's *Ginevra*, works by Vermeer and Monet, and a comprehenisve collection of American art. The massive building is accentuated by a large rotunda filled with flowers and the gentle sounds of a fountain, and by small garden courts in each wing of the building. The National Gallery frequently draws and creates some of the nation's finest temporary exhibits.

East Building Connected to the West Building by an underground plaza, this architectural masterpiece was created by the designer of the Louvre Pyramid, I. M. Pei (b.1917), and opened in 1978. The building's atrium contains a massive mobile designed by Alexander Calder (1898–1976). The galleries focus on 20th-century art, including the works of Henri Matisse, Andy Warhol, Pablo Picasso and Jackson Pollock. The galleries of the East Building are under renovation and will reopen in spring 2016.

THE BASICS

www.nga.gov
➕ H6
✉ Entrances on the Mall, on 7th Street, Constitution Avenue, 6th Street and 4th Street
☎ 202/737–4215
🕐 Mon–Sat 10–5, Sun 11–6
♿ Free
♿ Excellent
🍴 Pavilion Café, Garden Café
🚇 Archives-Navy Memorial, Judiciary, Smithsonian
❓ Tours daily

HIGHLIGHTS

● East Wing
● *Venus and Adonis*, Titian
● *The Alba Madonna*, Raphael
● *Laocoön*, El Greco
● *Daniel in the Lion's Den*, Peter Paul Rubens
● *Woman Holding a Balance*, Johannes Vermeer
● *A Girl with a Watering Can*, Auguste Renoir
● *Woman with a Parasol—Madame Monet and her Son*, Claude Monet
● *The Skater*, Gilbert Stuart

National Museum of the American Indian

The futuristic exterior (left); traditional shirt (middle); the rotunda display (right)

THE MALL TOP 25

THE BASICS

www.nmai.si.edu

✚ H7

✉ 4th Street SW and Independence Avenue

☎ 202/633-1000

🕐 Daily 10–5.30

💷 Free

♿ Excellent

Ⓜ L'Enfant Plaza

HIGHLIGHTS

● Limestone exterior and "grandfather rocks"
● Welcome Wall
● *Who We Are* video
● Wall of Gold
● 20ft (6m) totem pole by Nathan Jackson
● Light-filled atrium
● Navajo weavings
● ImagiNATIONS Activity Center

The first national museum dedicated to Native Americans, this Smithsonian building manages to pay homage to thousands of cultures with great cohesion. Well designed throughout, its exhibits are light years beyond traditional anthropological displays.

Connection to nature The exterior, fashioned out of Minnesota limestone, resembles a weatherworn rock mass, and the building sits on a serene 4.25-acre (1.7ha) plot with fountains and "grandfather rocks." Inside, light is refracted from a prism in the ceiling into the museum's five-floor "Potomac" atrium, which often plays host to traditonal ceremonies.

Break from tradition The museum breaks from the traditional anthropological treatment of Native Americans. "Our Universes" explores the spiritual relationship between humans and nature. "Our Peoples" documents the struggle to maintain a way of life in the face of adversity and aggression. The Wall of Gold has hundreds of gold objects from the 15th century. "Nation to Nation: Treaties between the United States and American Indian Nations" examines the history of US/American Indian diplomacy. The Red Power movement of the 1960s and '70s is highlighted. A large gallery space showcases the talents of Native American artists. The Lelawi Theater offers a spectacular video, *Who We Are*. The Rasmuson Theater features storytelling, dance and music presentations.

People visit the museum (left) to pay their respects at the displays (middle) and remember the lives lost (right)

US Holocaust Memorial Museum

This memorial to the millions of Jews and other targeted groups killed by the Nazis between 1933 and 1945 graphically portrays the personal stories and wider issues of persecution and human tragedy. The museum sets new standards for historical interpretation.

Disturbing "You cannot deal with the Holocaust as a reasonable thing," explained architect James Ingo Freed (1930–2005). To that end, he created a discordant building, intended to disturb the classical and sometimes placid facades elsewhere in Washington. Likewise, the central atrium, the Hall of Witness, disorients with twisted skylights, exposed load-bearing brick and architectural elements that don't join in conventional ways.

Nightmare Visitors are given identity cards that detail the life of a Holocaust victim as they enter a detailed history of the rise of anti-Semitism in Europe, the Nazi party and the machinations of the Holocaust. The brilliant and shocking displays are rendered using high-tech audiovisuals. Some viewers are moved to tears. The Hall of Remembrance, a place for quiet reflection, is a welcome respite at the end of the experience. A special exhibit for children under 12, "Daniel's Story," re-creates what life was like for a young boy trapped in the downward spiral of Nazi occupation. The Wexner Center, which holds temporary exhibitions, embodies the museum's forward-looking efforts to curb genocide.

THE BASICS

www.ushmm.org
🔢 G7
✉ 100 Wallenberg Place SW, south of Independence Avenue
☎ 202/488-0400
🕐 Daily 10–5.20. Closed Yom Kippur
🖐 Free
♿ Excellent
🍴 Vegetarian café
Ⓢ Smithsonian
❓ Mar–Aug free timed tickets distributed from 10am on a first come, first served basis; also available online in advance

---

HIGHLIGHTS

● Hall of Witness
● Hall of Remembrance
● For children (8–12): "Daniel's Story"

Washington Monument

HIGHLIGHTS

● Views from the top
● Museum at 490-foot level

TIPS

● Make reservations online in advance, even during the off season.
● Take a map of the city with you to the top so that you can point out your favorite places.
● Try to go at sunset to see the whole city painted in pastels.

An icon of Washington life, this monolith is the world's tallest masonry structure. The 70-second ride to the top is rewarded with a marvelous panorama over DC, Maryland and Virginia.

Rogues and cattle The Washington National Monument Society was founded in 1833 to solicit designs and funding for a memorial to America's first president. Construction began in 1848 but stopped in 1854 for over 20 years, in part because a rogue political party stole and destroyed a stone donated by the Pope. During this time, herds of Union cattle grazed on the grounds of the half-finished monument. A ring still betrays the slightly different marble that had to be used years later as construction began again amid the fervor

Clockwise from far left: The "Stars and Stripes" flying in the breeze below the Washington Monument; view from the top of the monument; the obelisk towering over the city of Washington; the monument reflected in the Tidal Basin; the Washington Monument and the Lincoln Memorial at dusk

surrounding the centennial of the American Revolution. In 1884, 36 years after the cornerstone was placed, a 6.28lb (2.85kg) aluminum point, at the time one of the world's most expensive metals, was placed on top of the 555ft (169m) monument, the tallest building in the world at that time.

View The observation deck, which opened in 2002, is 500ft (152m) above the ground. The views from the top cover most of Washington, as well as parts of Maryland and Virginia: look for the Tidal Basin, the Jefferson and Lincoln memorials, the White House, the US Capitol, the Library of Congress and the Smithsonian Institution. There are 193 commemorative stones donated by states, masonic lodges, church groups and foreign countries.

THE BASICS

www.nps.gov/wamo

🚩 F6

✉ The Mall at 15th Street NW

☎ 202/426–6841

🕐 Daily 9–4.45 (until 9.45 Memorial Day to Labor Day)

💲 $1.50 service charge per ticket if booked in advance, otherwise free on first come, first served basis. Get there early for timed tickets

♿ Excellent

Ⓜ Smithsonian

Vietnam Veterans Memorial

Glenna Goodacre sculpture (left); names of heroes on the black granite walls (right)

THE BASICS

www.nps.gov/vive

🔠 E6

✉ Near Constitution Avenue between 21st and 22nd Streets NW, adjacent to the Lincoln Memorial

☎ 202/426–6841

🕐 24 hours

💲 Free

♿ Excellent

🚇 Foggy Bottom, then 15-min walk

❓ Rangers available to assist in locating names

HIGHLIGHTS

● Inscribed names
● Frederick Hart's sculptural group
● Glenna Goodacre's sculptural group
● The city reflected in the polished stone

Opinions on this starkly simple sculpture have been as divided as those on the conflict that it commemorates. Some see it as the most moving memorial in Washington, while others have called it the "black gash of shame." What isn't in doubt is its popularity; on most days there is an almost constant procession of visitors.

Simple reminder Yale University student Maya Ying Lin (b.1959) was only 21 when she won the national design competition with a simple memorial—two triangular black granite walls, each 246ft (75m) long, set at a 125-degree angle and pointing toward the Washington Monument and Lincoln Memorial. The walls rise to 10ft (3m), seeming to overpower those who stand below. Names of heroes who made the ultimate sacrifice for their country are listed chronologically. Between 1959 and 1975 more than 58,000 were killed or reported missing in action.

A place to reflect The polished surface reflects sky, trees, nearby monuments and the faces of visitors searching for the names of loved ones. Each day National Park Service Rangers collect mementoes left near soldiers' names: letters, uniforms, military emblems, photographs. These tokens receive the same care as museum acquisitions. Some are on display at the American History Museum (▷ 50). In 1984 Frederick Hart's slightly larger-than-life sculpture of three soldiers was dedicated at the south entrance to the wall.

More to See

ALBERT EINSTEIN MEMORIAL

This bronze of Einstein, in a shaded elm grove at the National Academy of Sciences, is a pretty spot.
➕ E6 ✉ Constitution Avenue and 22nd Street NW 🕐 Free access Mon–Fri 9–5 🚇 Foggy Bottom–GWU and 10-min walk

BUREAU OF ENGRAVING AND PRINTING

www.moneyfactory.gov
Watch the powerful printing presses turn out millions of dollars every day.
➕ G7 ✉ 14 and C streets SW ☎ 866/874-2330 🕐 Visitor Center: Sep–Feb Mon–Fri 8.30–3.30; Mar–Aug 8.30–6.30 🚇 Smithsonian 💵 Free ❓ Tours every 15 min Sep–Feb 9–10.45, 12.30–2; Mar–Aug 9–10.45, 12.30–3.45, 5–6. Tickets required Mar–Aug. Booth on Raoul Wallenberg Place

DISCOVERY THEATER

www.discoverytheater.org
Smithsonian shows here include puppetry, music and storytelling.
➕ G7 ✉ 1100 Jefferson Drive SW ☎ 200/633-8700 🕐 Check online for schedule 🚇 Smithsonian 💵 Inexpensive

HIRSHHORN MUSEUM AND SCULPTURE GARDEN

www.hirshhorn.si.edu
This gallery showcases some first-rate art, including works by Henri Matisse, Man Ray and Andy Warhol.
➕ H7 ✉ 7th Street and Independence Avenue SW ☎ 202/633–4674 🕐 Daily 10–5.30, garden 7.30am–dusk 🚇 L'Enfant Plaza 💵 Free

KOREAN WAR VETERANS MEMORIAL

www.nps.gov/kowa
This memorial depicts 19 life-size figures marching through rugged terrain toward an American flag. The faces of 2,400 servicemen are etched into a wall nearby.
➕ E7 ✉ Between Lincoln Memorial and Independence Avenue ☎ 202/426–6841 🕐 Daily 24 hours 💵 Free

NATIONAL GALLERY OF ART SCULPTURE GARDEN

www.nga.gov
Many works by Louise Bourgeois, Joan Miró, Roy Lichtenstein and

The life-size figures of the Korean War Veterans Memorial

other 20th-century sculptors can be enjoyed in this garden.

✚ H6 ✉ Between Constitution Avenue and National Mall, 7th and 9th streets NW ☎ 202/737–4215 ⏱ Mon–Sat 10–5, Sun 11–6. Skating rink: winter daily hours vary 🍴 Pavilion Café Ⓜ Archives–Navy Memorial 🎫 Free. Skating moderate

NATIONAL MUSEUM OF AMERICAN HISTORY

www.americanhistory.si.edu

From Seinfeld's "puffy shirt" to inaugural ballgowns of the First Ladies, this museum, currently being renovated, is where you can find America's mementoes.

✚ G6 ✉ Constitution Avenue and 14th Street NW ☎ 202/633–1000 ⏱ Daily 10–5.30 Ⓜ Smithsonian, Federal Triangle 🎫 Free ❓ Tours

NATIONAL MUSEUM OF NATURAL HISTORY

www.mnh.si.edu

Dinosaurs and the Hope Diamond, fossils, millions of plant and animal specimens are all housed here.

✚ G6 ✉ Constitution Avenue and 10th Street NW ☎ 202/633–1000 ⏱ Daily 10–5.30 Ⓜ Smithsonian, Federal Triangle 🎫 Free

NATIONAL WORLD WAR II MEMORIAL

www.nps.gov/nwwm

Set on the axis between the Washington Monument and the Lincoln Memorial, this oval memorial commemorates the sacrifices made by Americans during World War II.

✚ F6 ✉ The Mall at 17th Street SW ☎ 202/426–6841 ⏱ Daily 24 hours Ⓜ Smithsonian, then 10-min walk 🎫 Free

OLD POST OFFICE BUILDING TOWER

www.nps.gov/opot

The clock tower here offers a dramatic view of the city. Closed until spring 2016 for renovation.

✚ G6 ✉ Pennsylvania Avenue at 12th Street NW ☎ 202/606–8691 ⏱ Opening hours under review 🍴 Many cafés and restaurants Ⓜ Federal Triangle 🎫 Free

The Old Post Office

Cartoon depicting jazz musician Duke Ellington, displayed in the National Museum of American History

Along the Mall

This walk along the grassy Mall will take you past DC's most famous landmarks and give you a good look at the soul of the city.

DISTANCE: 3 miles (4.8km) **ALLOW:** 3 hours

START

US CAPITOL (▷ 60–61)
✚ J6 🚇 Capitol South, Union Station

END

JEFFERSON MEMORIAL (▷ 36)
✚ F8 🚇 Smithsonian is a 15-min walk

❶ Start on the west steps of the Capitol. Look west toward the Washington Monument (▷ 46–47) across the green expanse of the National Mall, designed more than 200 years ago by Pierre L'Enfant.

❷ Descend the stairs, skirt the Reflecting Pool, and walk down the center of the Mall. This area is a center of activity for Washington. In summer Washingtonians play softball here and enjoy a wide range of festivals and the Independence Day celebration.

❸ As you walk down the Mall, you will pass the Smithsonian's greatest hits, along with the National Gallery of Art (▷ 43). Halfway down the Mall on your left is an old-fashioned carousel.

❹ As the Capitol grows smaller behind you, the Washington Monument has been growing larger. From its base you can see east back down the Mall and west to the Lincoln Memorial (▷ 38). From the top of the obelisk, you can see virtually the entire city.

❽ Less than a quarter mile down you will find the FDR Memorial (▷ 36). And, if you follow the path along the Tidal Basin another quarter mile, you will see the Jefferson Memorial (▷ 36).

❼ Near the Korean War Veterans Memorial (▷ 49), cross Independence Avenue and walk along the road until the sidewalk splits to the right. Follow the right fork around the Tidal Basin.

❻ Say hello to Abe, and then go and check out the Vietnam and Korean War memorials (▷ 48, 49) to the northeast and southeast.

❺ Walk west toward the Lincoln Memorial. Along the way you will pass the National World War II Memorial (▷ 50) and the Reflecting Pool, where crowds stood to listen to Martin Luther King, Jr. speak in 1963.

51

Shopping

NATIONAL AIR AND SPACE MUSEUM (▷ 40–41)

www.airandspace.si.edu
A three-floor temple to aviation and its knickknacks, this gift shop stocks "astronaut" food, toy rockets, model planes and kites.

✚ H7 ✉ Independence Avenue and 4th Street SW ☎ 202/633–2214 🕐 Daily 10–5.30 🚇 L'Enfant Plaza

NATIONAL GALLERY OF ART (▷ 43)

On the ground floor of the West Building, this gallery shop carries high-quality prints, art

stationery, scarves, ties and jewelry, along with other items dependent on the current traveling exhibition in the galleries housed above. Also gallery guides and catalogs.

✚ H6 ✉ 6th Street and Constitution Avenue NW ☎ 202/842–6002 🕐 Mon–Sat 10–5, Sun 11–6 🚇 Archives–Navy Memorial

NATIONAL MUSEUM OF THE AMERICAN INDIAN (▷ 44)

This museum's gift shop features high-grade textiles, jewelry, crafts and games made by Native American artisans.

✚ H7 ✉ 4th Street SW and Independence Avenue ☎ 202/633–7030 🕐 Daily 10–5.30 🚇 L'Enfant Plaza

NATIONAL MUSEUM OF NATURAL HISTORY (▷ 50)

www.mnh.si.edu
Five separate gift shops at this museum stock items ranging from dinosaur skeleton model kits to well-made jewelry and geodes.

✚ G6 ✉ Constitution Avenue and 10th Street NW ☎ 202/633–2060 🕐 Daily 10–5.30/6 🚇 Smithsonian

Restaurants

PRICES
Prices are approximate, based on a 3-course meal for one person.
$$$ over $50
$$ $30–$50
$ under $30

MITSITAM CAFÉ ($–$$)

www.mitsitamcafe.com
In the National Museum of the American Indian, this café offers a choice of Native American cuisines.

✚ H7 ✉ 4th Street and Independence Avenue SW ☎ 202/633–1000 🕐 Daily 11–5 🚇 L'Enfant Plaza

MUZE ($$$)

www.mandarinoriental.com/washington
Enjoy waterside views from this stylish restaurant

SEAFOOD SOUTHWEST

For a lively, colorful scene, head to the Southwest Fish Wharf (✚ G6 ✉ 1100 Maine Avenue SW), a floating seafood market at the Potomac River waterfront. From barges and boats, vendors hawk live blue crabs and a wide variety of fish; shucked shellfish, spiced shrimp and fried fish are available.

which serves international cuisine with the flavor of Southeast Asia.

✚ H7 ✉ 1330 Maryland Avenue SW ☎ 202/787–6148 🕐 Daily 11.30–2.30, 5.30–10 🚇 Smithsonian, then 10-min walk

PAVILION CAFÉ ($)

www.pavilioncafe.com
Pavilion serves up a tasty collection of paninis, wraps and salads.

✚ H6 ✉ Entrance via Constitution Avenue and Madison Drive at 9th Street NW ☎ 202/289–3361 🕐 Mon–Thu 10–7, Fri–Sat 10–9, Sun 11–7 🚇 Archives–Navy Memorial

Capitol Hill

Dominated by federal buildings, Capitol Hill is home to the Capitol building, Union Station, the Supreme Court and the Library of Congress. Neighborhoods of Victorian row houses stretch east from these buildings.

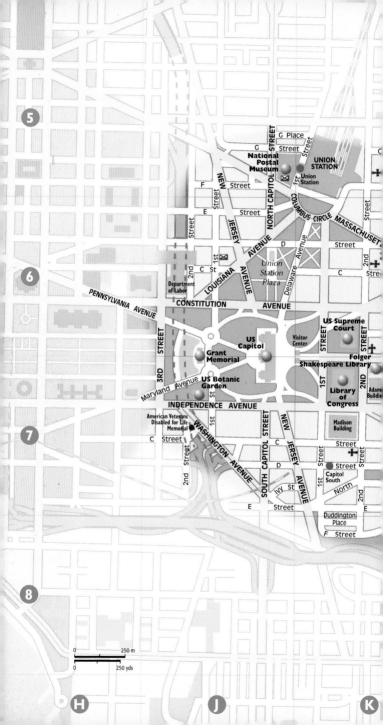

Library of Congress

Even in a city chockablock with archives and libraries, the Library of Congress is the mother lode. One of the world's largest libraries, the de facto national library contains more than 158 million items, in 470 languages, on 530 miles (853km) of shelves.

A universal approach Congress appropriated funds for a library in 1800, but it was destroyed by the British when they sacked the Capitol in 1814. Thomas Jefferson's personal library, one of the finest in the world, then became the nucleus of the new collection. Jefferson's universal approach to knowledge and book collection became the philosophy for the library itself, despite its intended purpose to be a resource for congresspeople and their staff. The library now files more than 12,000 new books a day, all copyrighted in the US. The library has also collected random historical items including the contents of Lincoln's pockets on the evening he was shot, original scores by Beethoven and Brahms, and props belonging to Houdini.

Room to read The Italian Renaissance Jefferson Building houses the library's Main Reading Room. A dozen figures representing the countries or empires that were pivotal in the creation of Western civilization look down from the apex of the 160ft (48.8m) dome. It is supported by columns topped by female figures representing the aspects of civilized life, including religion, commerce, history and art.

THE BASICS

www.loc.gov

➕ K7

✉ 1st Street and Independence Avenue SE

☎ 202/707–8000

🕐 Mon–Sat 8.30–4.30

🎟 Free

♿ Excellent. Visitor Services (☎ 202/707–9779) has American Sign Language interpretation

🍴 Cafeteria, coffee shop, snack bars

Ⓜ Capitol South

❓ Tours begin at the Jefferson Building Mon–Sat 10.30, 11.30, 12.30, 1.30, 2.30, 3.30 (Sat no 12.30 and 3.30 tours). Resources are open to over-16s pursuing research

HIGHLIGHTS

● Torch of Learning on green copper dome
● Beaux Arts design
● Main Reading Room
● Sculpture inside and out
● View of the Capitol from the Madison Building cafeteria

US Botanic Garden

HIGHLIGHTS

● Seasonal displays
● Orchids and tropical plants
● Coffee, chocolate and banyan trees
● Bartholdi Fountain

TIPS

● The titan arum (corpse flower) last flowered in 2013 and was captured on a live webcam.
● Make sure you wear layers as the temperature in the glasshouse's rooms are set to suit the plants, not necessarily you.

A microcosm of climates in the US, the Botanic Garden lets you experience the desert of Arizona even when it's cold out, and blooms flower all year. December's poinsettia display is a crowd pleaser.

Exotic glasshouse plants In 1838, Congress authorized Lieutenant Charles Wilkes, a surly captain said to be the inspiration for Melville's Captain Ahab, and his crew to circle the globe so that they might provide more accurate charts for the whaling industry. Wilkes returned in 1842 with a collection of exotic plant species, and Congress rekindled dormant plans for a botanical garden. The present conservatory, an attractive combination of iron-and-glass greenhouse and stone orangeries, was erected in 1933. Following a four-year, $33.5 million

A tall cactus in the massive glasshouse at the US Botanic Garden (left); a tranquil escape from the crowds on the Mall, the Conservatory houses lush tropical plants and trees (right)

renovation, the garden is now home to more than 65,000 plants.

Flowers for all seasons The main entrance hall serves as a seasonal gallery displaying by turns Christmas poinsettias, tulips and hyacinths, or chrysanthemums. The conservatory's 14 viewing areas feature plants grown for different uses and in different environments—from high desert flora to the jungle and from coffee and chocolate trees to plants that help us fight cancer. Tucked in the gardens are four specimens—the Vessel Fern, the Ferocious Blue Cycad and two Sago Palms—that are believed to be directly related to those brought back on the Wilkes expedition. The fountain in an adjacent park was sculpted by Frederic Bartholdi, designer of the Statue of Liberty.

THE BASICS

www.usbg.gov

♦ J7

✉ 1st Street SW and Independence Avenue (100 Maryland Avenue SW)

☎ 202/225-8333

🕐 Conservatory and National Garden daily 10–5. Bartholdi Park dawn to dusk

🎟 Free

♿ Excellent

🚇 Federal Center SW

US Capitol

TOP 25

HIGHLIGHTS

- Rotunda
- Frescoes by Constantino Brumidi
- Paintings by John Trumbull
- Visit to the House or Senate Chambers (not part of the Capitol tour—separate pass required)

TIP

- Be aware that the dome is undergoing restoration and is partly obscured. Work should be completed in 2016.

The Capitol dome is an iconic backdrop for newscasters and politicians as a symbol of American democracy. A state-of-the-art underground visitor center tells you more.

Icon The 4,500-ton, cast-iron dome was an engineering feat when undertaken in 1851 by Capitol architect Thomas U. Walter and US Army Quartermaster Captain Montgomery Meigs. It became a political symbol before it was even half finished: The Civil War broke out while it was under construction, and the Capitol housed the wounded. Many advised President Lincoln to halt work on the building, but he was adamant that progress continue as "a sign we intend the Union shall go on." The dome was completed in 1868.

Clockwise from far left: The famous dome of the US Capitol; visitors inspecting the Rotunda; the Capitol is visible from nearly every part of the city, as it stands at the very heart of Washington; the columns of the Capitol; classical figures adorning the Capitol's exterior

Founding Fathers Visitors to the Capitol can tour the old Supreme Court Chamber where famous cases have been decided; Statuary Hall, where the House of Representatives first met; the old Senate Chamber, where Webster, Clay and Calhoun famously sparred; and the ornate Brumidi Corridors (special tour Mon–Fri 2pm). But the crowning moment of the tour is the Rotunda, under the Capitol dome. Eight gigantic murals, four by George Washington's aide John Trumbull, depict scenes from the colonies and the revolutionary period. *The Apotheosis of Washington*, visible through the eye of the inner dome, depicts classical deities surrounding the first president. Constantino Brumidi (1805–80), who painted the fresco, was said to consort with "ladies of the night," whose likenesses then appeared in the painting.

THE BASICS

www.visitthecapitol.gov

✚ J6

✉ East Capitol and 1st Street

☎ 202/226–8000

🕐 Mon–Sat 8.30–4.30

💵 Free

♿ Excellent

🍴 Restaurant

🚇 Capitol South, Union Station, Federal Center

❓ Tours run Mon–Sat 8.50–3.10 and are free but require passes. US citizens can ask their elected representatives; anyone can book online. A limited number of same-day passes are available daily at the information desks at the Visitor Center. Don't bring large bags such as backpacks as they are prohibited

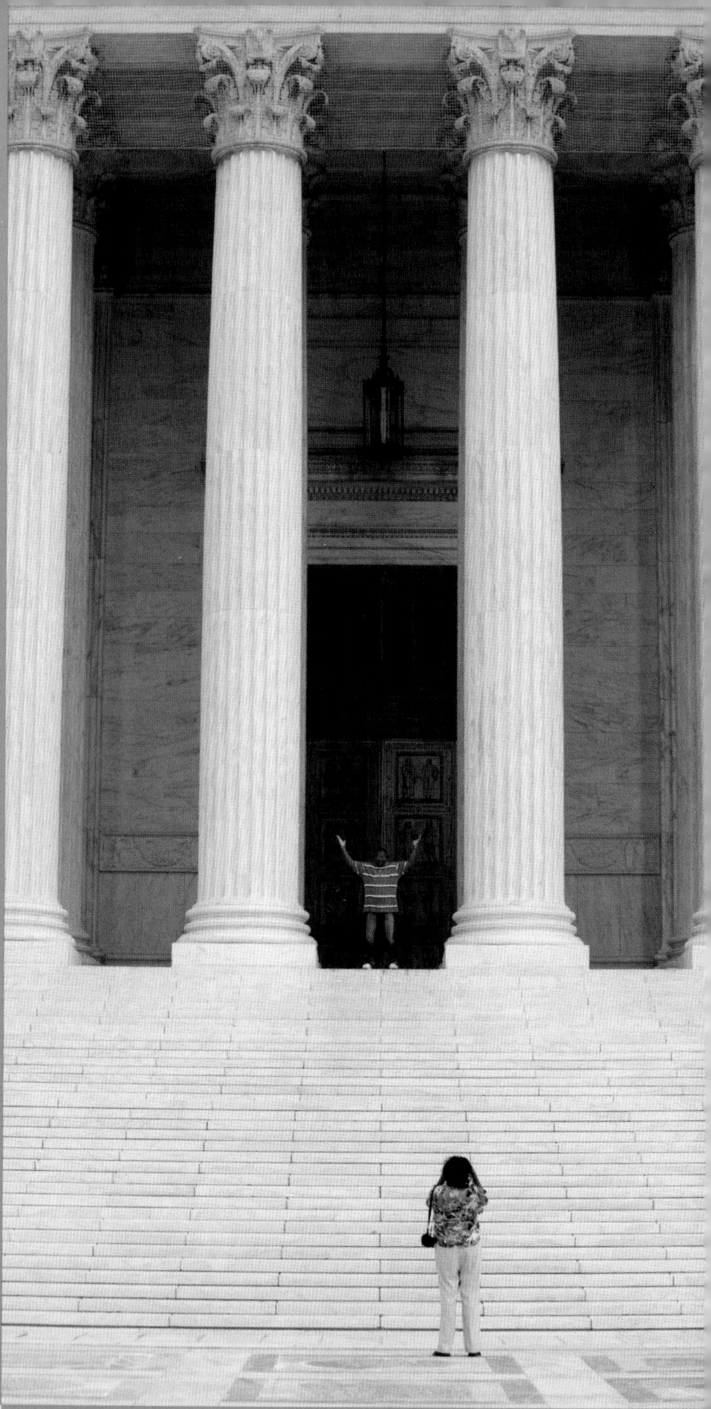

US Supreme Court Building

Exterior of the US Supreme Court (left and below); detail of Contemplation of Justice *(right)*

One justice called this 1935 neoclassical building, designed by Cass Gilbert, Jr., "bombastically pretentious…for a quiet group of old boys such as the Supreme Court."

Judgments America's highest court may still be "old boy," despite the arrival of Justice Elena Kagan—only the fourth woman to serve on the court in its 226-year history—but it has never been quiet. The 1857 Dred Scott decision, which held that Congress had no authority to limit slavery, contributed to the onset of the Civil War. Rulings on abortion have frequently made the plaza in front of the building a focus of civil disobedience. *Brown v. Board of Education* required the integration of schools and bus travel across the land and *Engel v. Vitale* outlawed school prayer. The justices, who are appointed for life, seldom give interviews.

Law in action The steps up to the colonnaded entrance are flanked by two white-marble allegorical figures by James Earle Fraser, depicting *The Contemplation of Justice* and *The Authority of Law*. The magnificent bronze entrance doors lead into an entrance hall adorned with busts of all the former chief justices. When the court is in session you can join the "three-minute line" and glimpse proceedings from the Standing Gallery. A statue of John Marshall, Chief Justice from 1755 to 1835, dominates the street level where a short film and changing exhibits describe the work of the court.

THE BASICS

www.supremecourt.gov
⊞ K6
✉ 1st and East Capitol streets NE
☎ 202/479–3030
⏰ Mon–Fri 9–4.30
💷 Free
♿ Excellent
🍴 Cafeteria
Ⓜ Capitol South, Union Station
❓ Lectures on the half-hour when the court is not in session 9.30–3.30

HIGHLIGHTS

● Bronze entrance doors
● Plaza sculpture
● Busts of chief justices
● Film and exhibits on Court history
● The court in session

More to See

EASTERN MARKET

www.easternmarket-dc.org
Renovated after a fire in 2007, this fresh food market has been in continuous operation since 1873. Local artisan wares, too (▷ 66).
➕ L7 ✉ 225 7th Street SE ⏱ Tue–Fri 7–7, Sat 7–6, Sun 9–5 🚇 Eastern Market

FOLGER SHAKESPEARE LIBRARY

www.folger.edu
The world's most comprehensive collection of Shakespeare's works is part of this library of 275,000-plus books, manuscripts and paintings from and about the European Renaissance.
➕ K7 ✉ 201 E Capitol Street SE ☎ 202/544-7077 ⏱ Mon–Sat 10–5, Sun 12–5. Garden tours Apr–Oct every 1st and 3rd Sat 🚇 Capitol South 💵 Free; theater performances expensive

FREDERICK DOUGLASS MUSEUM

www3.nahc.org/fd/
The first Washington home of one of the country's most celebrated abolitionists now houses two rooms of Douglass memorabilia and the Hall of Fame for Caring Americans.
➕ K6 ✉ 320 A Street NE ☎ 202/547-4273 ⏱ Tours of house by appointment only 🚇 Union Station

GRANT MEMORIAL

Cool and calm Ulysses S. Grant, Civil War general and former president, is honored atop his horse in this memorial, the third largest equestrian statue in the world.
➕ J6 ✉ 1st Street NW at foot of Capitol Hill ⏱ Daily 24 hours 🚇 Federal Center SW 💵 Free

NATIONAL POSTAL MUSEUM

www.postalmuseum.si.edu
Tributes to the Pony Express, 11 million stamps and interactive exhibits illuminate the history of the US Postal Service in this family-oriented museum.
➕ J5 ✉ 2 Massachusetts Avenue NE across from Union Station ☎ 202/633-5555 ⏱ Daily 10–5.30 🚇 Union Station 💵 Free

The Grant Memorial

Federal Route

Capitol Hill is where you can get closest to the action. Take this walk to catch a glimpse of a Congressional staffer's daily life.

DISTANCE: 1.75 miles (2.8km) **ALLOW:** 2 hours

START .... END

US CAPITOL (▷ 60–61)
✚ J6 🚇 Capitol South, Union Station, Federal Center

EASTERN MARKET OR BARRACKS ROW (▷ 64) ✚ L7 🚇 Eastern Market

❶ Start at US Capitol (▷ 60–61) on Delaware Avenue. On the way you will pass the Russell Senate Office Building, where many Senators' offices and their staff are housed.

❼ From here you can enjoy some lively shopping at Eastern Market (▷ 64, 66), north on 7th Street, or stop for food and drinks on the quickly gentrifying Barracks Row, south on 8th Street.

❷ If you don't have time to go inside the Capitol, take time to walk around it. Head west after you cross Constitution Avenue and follow the large circular path around the front of the Capitol.

❻ Depending on the time of day, you will see congressional staff grabbing a quick lunch or relaxing after a long day in the bars and restaurants that line the south side of Pennsylvania Avenue. Continue to the Eastern Market Metro stop.

❸ You will pass the Peace Monument before reaching the Grant Memorial (▷ 64) due west of the Capitol. Take the opportunity to climb the stairs for a view down the Mall toward the Washington Monument (▷ 46–47).

❺ The path ends at 1st Street SE and Independence Avenue. Taking Independence east you will pass the buildings of the Library of Congress (▷ 57) before turning right on Pennsylvania Avenue.

❹ Walk back down the stairs and continue south on the path around the Capitol. You will pass the Garfield Memorial and the US Botanic Garden (▷ 58–59) before heading up the hill, with the House Office Buildings on your right.

Shopping

A. LITTERI

www.alitteri.com
In the heart of the wholesale market since 1932, this Italian shop stocks more than 100 types of olive oils and wines to go with any pasta dish you can dream up.
✚ L4 ✉ 517 Morse Street NE ☎ 202/544-0183
🕓 Tue–Wed 8–4, Thu 8–5, Fri–Sat 8–6 🚇 New York Avenue

CAPITOL HILL BOOKS

www.capitolhillbooks-dc.com
It's near impossible for this store to stock any more used books. Don't yodel too loud—you might find yourself crushed under an avalanche of foreign language books in the bathroom. Seriously.
✚ L7 ✉ 657 C Street SE ☎ 202/544-1621 🕓 Mon–Fri 11.30–6, Sat–Sun 9–6
🚇 Eastern Market

DAWN PRICE BABY

www.dawnpricebaby.com
Toys and clothes for tots are the specialty here.
✚ L7 ✉ 325 7th Street SE ☎ 202/543-2920 🕓 Mon–Fri 11–6, Sat–Sun 10–5
🚇 Eastern Market

EASTERN MARKET

www.easternmarket-dc.org
Here you'll find fresh produce under the canopy on weekends and fresh meats, fish, cheeses, baked goods and prepared foods (especially Mexican and Italian) six days a week. Saturday also brings a craft market, with a large selection of handmade jewelry.
✚ L7 ✉ 225 7th Street SE 🕓 Tue–Fri 7–7, Sat 7–6, Sun 9–5 🚇 Eastern Market

FAIRY GODMOTHER

This specialty store caters to children of all ages, with a multicultural choice of books and toys.
✚ L7 ✉ 319 7th Street SE ☎ 202/547-5474 🕓 Mon–Fri 10.30–6, Sat 10–5, Sun 10.30–3.30 🚇 Eastern Market

FORECAST

www.forecaststore.com
Well known for its excellent service and stylish, classic clothing for women, Forecast also stocks homewares and accessories.
✚ L7 ✉ 218 7th Street SE ☎ 202/547-7337
🕓 Tue–Fri 11–7, Sat 10–6, Sun 12–5 🚇 Eastern Market

GROOVY DC CARDS & GIFTS

www.groovydc.com
A quirky card and gift shop with lovely items like journals, photo frames, candles, prints and local art.
✚ L7 ✉ 321 7th Street SE ☎ 202/544-6633
🕓 Mon 12–6, Tue–Fri 11–7, Sat 10–6, Sun 11–5
🚇 Eastern Market

PAPYRUS

www.papyrusonline.com
Great selection of greetings cards, stationery, gifts and gift wrapping in a gallery-style setting in Union Station.
✚ K5 ✉ 50 Massachusetts Avenue NE ☎ 202/551-0757
🕓 Mon–Fri 7am–9pm, Sat 9–9, Sun 10–7 🚇 Union Station

UNION STATION

www.unionstationdc.com
The city's main railway station and transportation hub also doubles as a shopping mall where you can wander along marble-floored avenues under vaulted ceilings.
✚ K5 ✉ 50 Massachusetts Avenue NE ☎ 202/289-1908
🕓 Mon–Sat 10–9, Sun 12–6
🚇 Union Station

WOVEN HISTORY AND SILK ROAD

www.wovenhistory.com
Selling Persian and tribal textiles, weavings and rugs, owner Mamet will "charm and disarm" you with his travels and tales, and stories of how he has set up looms in refugee camps.
✚ L7 ✉ 315 7th Street SE ☎ 202/543-1705 🕓 Tue–Sun 10–6 🚇 Eastern Market

MARKET MENU

For fresh produce and artisanal meats, check out Eastern Market (▷ 64 and left), Dupont Circle Market (Q Street NW and Massachusetts Avenue; Jan–Mar Sun 10am–1pm, Mar–Dec Sun 9am–2pm), or the Adams-Morgan Farmers Market (18th Street NW and Columbia Road; May–Dec Sat 8–2).

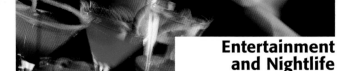

Entertainment and Nightlife

CAPITOL LOUNGE
www.capitolloungedc.com
Popular among Hill staffers, "Cap Lounge" is also for those hoping to catch a soccer match on TV.
➕ K7 ✉ 229 Pennsylvania Avenue SE ☎ 202/547–2098 🕐 Mon–Wed 4pm–2am, Thu 11am–2am, Fri 11am–3am, Sat–Sun 10.30am–3am 🚇 Capitol South

COOLIDGE AUDITORIUM
www.loc.gov
With its near-perfect acoustics and sightlines, this Library of Congress auditorium draws talented musicians from a broad range of genres.
➕ K7 ✉ 101 Independence Avenue SE ☎ 202/707–5502 🚇 Capitol South

THE DUBLINER
www.dublinerdc.com
This Irish pub, a favorite with Senate staff, often features live music.

SPECTATOR SPORTS
If you are here in fall (autumn), you will hear about the Redskins American football team, but season-ticket holders have all the seats. It's easier to see the Wizards play basketball or the Capitals play hockey, both at the Verizon Center in downtown Washington. Look online for single ticket sales or try www.stubhub.com/washington-redskins-tickets

➕ J5 ✉ 4 F Street NW ☎ 202/737–3773 🕐 Sun–Thu 11am–1.30am, Fri–Sat 11am–2.30am 🚇 Union Station

FOLGER SHAKESPEARE LIBRARY
www.folger.edu
Daring productions of the Bard's work are staged here in this re-creation of an Elizabethan theater.
➕ K7 ✉ 201 East Capitol Street SE ☎ 202/544–4600 🚇 Capitol South

HAWK'N'DOVE
www.hawkndovedc.com
This dark-wood-panel bar is frequented by lobbyists, politicos and interns.
➕ K7 ✉ 329 Pennsylvania Avenue SE ☎ 202/547–0030 🕐 Mon–Thu 11am–2am, Fri 11am–3am, Sat 10am–3am, Sun 10am–2am 🚇 Capitol South

LOCKHEED MARTIN IMAX THEATER
www.si.edu/imax
The giant IMAX screeen at the National Air and Space Museum (▷ 40–41) shows larger-than-life nature, wildlife and space films.
➕ H7 ✉ 6th Street and Independence Avenue SW ☎ 866/868–7444 🕐 Check for times 🚇 L'Enfant Plaza

SONOMA WINE BAR
www.sonomadc.com
A soothing bar with exposed brick walls and hardwood floors, Sonoma offers a large selection of wine by the glass and a knowledgeable staff.
➕ K7 ✉ 223 Pennsylvania Avenue SE ☎ 202/544–8088 🕐 Dinner daily, lunch Mon–Fri 🚇 Capitol South

TORTILLA COAST
www.tortillacoast.com
Solid Tex-Mex and well-priced margaritas by the pitcher pull droves of young Hill staffers to this watering hole right after work.
➕ K7 ✉ 400 1st Street SE ☎ 202/546–6768 🕐 Mon–Wed, Sat 11–10, Thu–Fri 11–11, Sun 11–9 🚇 Capitol South

TUNE IN
Enjoy a cold beer or an all-day breakfast in this booth-lined bar over-looked by a selection of stuffed animal heads.
➕ K7 ✉ 331 Pennsylvania Avenue SE ☎ 202/542–2725 🕐 Mon–Fri 8am–2am, Sat–Sun 8am–3am 🚇 Capitol South

MOVIES
Check the daily newspapers for mainstream first-run movies. For art-house and foreign films, try **Landmark's Bethesda Row Cinema** (☎ 301/652–7273) or **Landmark's E Street Cinema** (☎ 202/783–9494). The **Library of Congress** (☎ 202/707–9779) often shows old movies at various locations, including some silent films.

Restaurants

PRICES

Prices are approximate, based on a 3-course meal for one person.

$$$	over $50
$$	$30–$50
$	under $30

BANANA CAFÉ AND PIANO BAR ($)

www.bananacafedc.com
Stick with the Cuban and Puerto Rican dishes at this lively, colorful eatery that features live entertainment each night.
✚ L8 ✉ 500 8th Street SE
☎ 202/543–5906 🕐 Daily lunch, dinner 🚇 Eastern Market

BELGA CAFÉ ($–$$)

www.belgacafe.com
This smart Belgian restaurant is best at brunch with its unique, but subtly flavored, options, including goat cheese waffles with red pepper coulis and poached eggs with salmon and asparagus.
✚ L8 ✉ 514 8th Street SE
☎ 202/544–0100
🕐 Daily dinner, Mon–Fri lunch, Sat–Sun brunch
🚇 Eastern Market

BISTRO BIS ($$–$$$)

www.bistrobis.com
In the Hotel George, Bis offers an extensive wine list to complement its solid French menu. The warm and elegant environment draws power players, celebrities and senators.
✚ J6 ✉ 15 E Street NW
☎ 202/661–2700 🕐 Daily breakfast, lunch and dinner 🚇 Union Station

CHARLIE PALMER STEAK ($$$)

www.charliepalmer.com/charlie-palmer-steak-dc
This sleek restaurant with a view of the Capitol is known for its high-power clientele and quality steaks masterfully prepared by chef Jeffery Russell.
✚ J6 ✉ 101 Constitution Avenue NW ☎ 202/547–8100 🕐 Mon–Fri lunch and dinner, Sat dinner 🚇 Union Station

FIREHOOK ($)

www.firehook.com
This popular bakery churns out tasty sandwiches on fresh-baked bread, along with an array of tarts, pies, muffins, pastries and fresh salads.
✚ K7 ✉ 215 Pennsylvania Avenue SE ☎ 202/429–2253

UNION STATION

Alongside the train services and shopping opportunities, you'll find a huge variety of eating places at Union Station (▷ 66). There are restaurants serving American, Japanese, Mexican, Korean, Filipino, Chinese and Indian cuisine, and there are plenty of places to stop for a coffee, a tasty light lunch or a fast-food option.

🕐 Mon–Fri 6.30am–7pm, Sat–Sun 7–5 🚇 Capitol South

LA LOMA ($–$$)

www.lalomarestaurantdc.com
The Mexican cuisine may not be too hot, but the gossip-filled whisperings of congressional staff is enough to satisfy.
✚ K6 ✉ 316 Massachusetts Avenue NE ☎ 202/548–2550 🕐 Daily lunch, dinner 🚇 Union Station

MARKET LUNCH ($)

This counter-service eatery in the Eastern Market features crab cakes, fried fish and North Carolina barbecue.
✚ L6 ✉ 225 7th Street SE
☎ 202/547–8444 🕐 Tue–Fri 7.30–2.30, Sat 8–3, Sun 11–3 🚇 Eastern Market

THE MONOCLE RESTAURANT ($$–$$$)

www.themonocle.com
A steak and seafood restaurant across the street from the Senate office building.
✚ K6 ✉ 107 D Street NE
☎ 202/546–4488 🕐 Mon–Fri 11.30am–midnight 🚇 Union Station

MONTMARTRE ($$)

www.montmartredc.com
A traditional but exceptional French bistro with an open kitchen and friendly environment.
✚ L6 ✉ 327 7th Street SE
☎ 202/544–1244 🕐 Tue–Sun lunch, dinner, Sat–Sun brunch 🚇 Eastern Market

DC's wealthiest neighborhood first became popular in the 1960s and has grown more affluent ever since. A perfect spot for outdoor shopping, Georgetown brings droves in the warmer months.

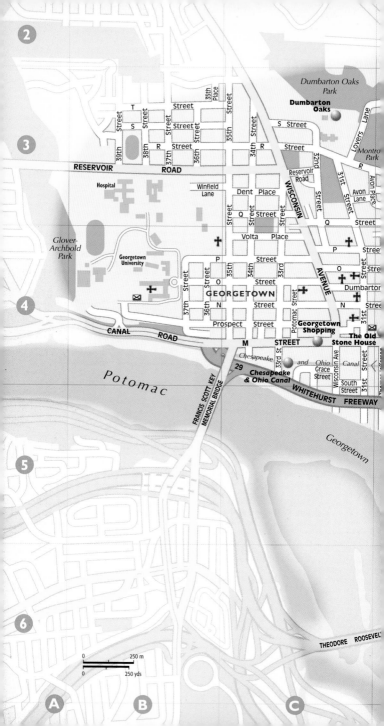

Georgetown Shopping

Jackie Kennedy first drew the rich and powerful to Georgetown with the cocktail parties she held during her husband's time in the US Senate. Her guests stayed, populating the Federalist town houses that line this neighborhood's narrow tree-lined streets. Inevitably, Georgetown quickly became, and has remained, DC's upscale shopping destination.

Wisconsin and M Metro inaccessibility does not deter crowds from Georgetown's main intersection, full of chic shops that stretch north on Wisconsin Avenue and east on M Street. Warm months are particularly busy as tourists and locals flock to the shops they know—Banana Republic, Urban Outfitters and Coach, among countless others. An indoor mall on the southwest corner of the intersection, The Shops at Georgetown, with J. Crew, Ann Taylor, Anthropologie and H&M, is equally popular.

Not just an outdoor mall You'll also find boutiques, antiques shops, home furnishings and bookstores. Dubbed "Georgetown's Design District," Cady's Alley, off 33rd Street just south of M Street, is lined with mid- to high-end home furnishing galleries. Georgetown's fine antiques shops can be found mainly on the eastern section of M Street before it crosses Rock Creek Parkway. Some of the better independent shops huddle farther up Wisconsin Avenue on Book Hill, just south of the Georgetown Library.

THE BASICS

✚ C4
✉ Mainly M Street NW between 30th Street and 34th Street and Wisconsin Avenue NW between South Street and R Street
♿ Limited

HIGHLIGHTS

● The Shops at Georgetown
● A stroll along the C&O Canal towpath
● The view from the Georgetown Library
● Wandering among the Federalist mansions to the northeast of the intersection between Wisconsin Avenue and M Street

John F. Kennedy Center

Bust of Kennedy inside the Kennedy Center (left) and the Hall of Nations (right)

THE BASICS

www.kennedy-center.org

➕ D6

✉ 2700 F Street NW

☎ 202/416–8340; 800/444–1324

🕐 Tours every 10 min Mon–Fri 10–5, Sat–Sun 10–1

💲 Free tours; performance ticket prices vary

⚐ Excellent

🍴 K. C. Café, Roof Terrace Restaurant ☎ 202/416– 8555 for reservations 🕐 Café daily 11.30–8; restaurant dinner 5–8 before performances; brunch 11–2 most Sun

🚇 Foggy Bottom. Free bus shuttle every 15 min Mon–Fri 9.45am–midnight, Sat 10am–midnight, Sun 12–12

❓ Free 1-hour tours Mon–Fri 10–5, Sat–Sun 10–1. Free Millennium Stage performance daily at 6pm

HIGHLIGHTS

- Hall of States
- View from the roof terrace
- Henri Matisse tapestries
- Well-stocked gift shop

With seven theaters, this national cultural center covers 8 acres (3.2ha) and is the jewel of the city's arts scene. The roof terrace provides a stunning 360-degree view of Washington and the Potomac.

The seat of the arts Opened in 1971, Edward Durell Stone's white-marble box overlooks the Potomac River next to the Watergate complex. In 1958, when President Eisenhower (1890– 1969) signed the National Cultural Center Act, it was the first time that the US government financed a structure dedicated to the performing arts. As a living memorial to President Kennedy, and subsequently a beneficiary of federal funding, the center is still a unique public-private partnership. It now hosts more than 3,000 performances a year by some of the world's most talented artists. A major expansion project started in December 2014.

Hall of States The red carpet in the Hall of States and the parallel Hall of Nations leads to the Grand Foyer, where visitors are greeted by a 3,000lb (1,363kg) bronze bust of President Kennedy. This 630ft (192m) long hall blazes from the light of 16 Orrefors crystal chandeliers, donated by Sweden and reflected in 58ft-high (17.7m) mirrors, a gift from Belgium. One end of the hall is devoted to the Millennium Stage, where free performances are given every evening. The building also contains an opera house, a concert hall, two stage theaters, a jazz club and a theater lab.

More to See

CHESAPEAKE & OHIO CANAL
www.nps.gov/choh

This tree-lined canal runs parallel to the Potomac River from Georgetown to Cumberland, Maryland. Mule-drawn canal boats are operated by the National Park Service from the Great Falls visitor center in Potomac, MD.

🚩 C4 ⊠ C&O Canal Visitor Center: 1057 Thomas Jefferson Street NW ☎ Canal boat rides 301/767–3714 (Sat, Sun 11, 1.30, 3) ⏰ Visitor Center: Wed–Sun 9–4.30 (summer only) 🚇 Foggy Bottom, then 15-min walk 🖑 Free. Canal boat tour moderate; under 3 free

DUMBARTON OAKS
www.doaks.org

In 1944, the international conference leading to the formation of the United Nations was held at this estate, also known for its formal garden, with an orangery, rose garden, wisteria and shaded terraces. This a must for anyone interested in gardens or who likes to be surrounded by blazing nature.

🚩 C3 ⊠ 31st and R streets NW ☎ 202/ 339–6401 ⏰ Museum daily 11.30–5.30; garden 2–6 (closes 5pm Nov–14 Mar 🚇 Dupont Circle, then bus D2 or DC Circulator bus 🖑 Garden moderate; museum free

KREEGER MUSEUM
www.kreegermuseum.org

Built by David and Carmen Kreeger, this Philip Johnson mansion now houses art, mainly the work of male masters of the last two centuries.

🚩 Off map at A2 ⊠ 2401 Foxhall Road NW ☎ 202/338–3552 ⏰ Tue–Thu tours 10.30, 1.30 (reservations required), Fri–Sat 10–4 (no reservations required) 🚇 Tenleytown, then taxi or walk 🖑 Expensive

THE OLD STONE HOUSE
www.nps.gov/olst

The oldest house in the city, dating from 1765, commemorates the daily lives of the early residents of Georgetown.

🚩 D4 ⊠ 3051 M Street NW ☎ 202/894– 6070 ⏰ Daily 11–6 🚇 Foggy Bottom, then 15-min walk 🖑 Free

Towpath of the Chesapeake & Ohio Canal

The oldest house in Washington, the Old Stone House

Waterfront Walk

See one of Washington's oldest and most stately neighborhoods from a variety of angles and perspectives.

DISTANCE: 1.5 miles (2.4km) **ALLOW:** 2 hours

START

JOHN F. KENNEDY CENTER
(▷ 74) ✚ D6 Ⓜ Foggy Bottom

END

GEORGETOWN UNIVERSITY
✚ B4 Ⓜ Rosslyn (a 20-min walk)

❶ Start with a view of the Georgetown waterfront from the terrace of the Kennedy Center (▷ 74).

❽ Heading left on Volta Street will take you to the Georgetown University Campus. The Georgetown Library is 0.25 miles (0.4km) farther up Wisconsin Avenue. From the small park behind the library you get a great view over Georgetown.

❷ Exit through the front of the building; take a left and then another left onto F Street. Cross the parkway that runs under the Kennedy Center Terrace and turn right on the path by the Potomac.

❼ Turn right on Wisconsin Avenue and follow it up the hill. Washington DC's most expensive houses sit on the tree-lined streets to your right.

❸ Follow the Potomac north and catch a glimpse of the infamous Watergate Hotel on your right. The path curves behind the boathouse and then back to the river.

❻ Take a left on M Street. You are now entering the shopping district (▷ 73), the epicenter of which is at Wisconsin Avenue and M Street.

❹ Stroll on the boardwalk past the restaurants and bars along the Georgetown waterfront. Then take a right on the edge of the park and cross onto 31st Street. The movie theater on your left used to be the Georgetown incinerator.

❺ Continue up the hill on 31st Street, crossing over the C&O Canal (▷ 75). You will see Georgetown's old mills to the west. That smokestack was once part of a paper mill.

A MANO

www.amano.bz

A Mano ("By Hand") stocks fine home furnishings crafted by European artisans.

➕ C3 ✉ 1677 Wisconsin Avenue NW ☎ 202/298–7200 🕐 Mon–Sat 10–6, Sun 12–5

ANTHROPOLOGIE

www.anthropologie.com

A magnet of shabby chic carrying homewares, clothing and accessories.

➕ C4 ✉ 3222 M Street NW ☎ 202/337–1363 🕐 Mon–Sat 10–9, Sun 12–7

BRIDGE STREET BOOKS

www.bridgestreetbooks.com

This charming row house contains a good collection of books.

➕ D4 ✉ 2814 Pennsylvania Avenue NW ☎ 202/965–5200 🕐 Mon–Thu 11–9, Fri–sat 11–10, Sun 12–6

DESIGN WITHIN REACH

www.dwr.com

Modern home furnishings from well-known designers from around the world set in gallery displays.

➕ C4 ✉ 3307 Cady's Alley, 3306 M Street NW ☎ 202/339–9480 🕐 Mon–Sat 10–6, Sun 12–6

HU'S SHOES

www.husonline.com

On the absolute front edge of fashion, Hu's carries shoes you can't find outside of New York, Paris or Milan.

➕ D4 ✉ 3005 M Street NW (also at 2906 M Street) ☎ 202/342–0202/342–2020 🕐 Mon–Sat 10–7, Sun 12–5

INTERMIX

www.intermixonline.com

Intermix offers hand-picked styles from the "it" list of designers, including the UK's popular Stella McCartney.

➕ C4 ✉ 3300 M Street NW ☎ 202/298–8080 🕐 Mon–Sat 11–8, Sun 12–6

JEAN PIERRE ANTIQUES

www.jeanpierreantiques.com

There's no need to go to France: Enjoy this Georgetown shop that supplies antique furniture to well-heeled locals and famous visitors.

➕ D4 ✉ 2601 P Street NW ☎ 202/337–1731 🕐 Mon–Fri 11–5, Sat–Sun 12–5

JUST PAPER AND TEA

www.justpaperandtea.com

Home to a large selection of fine paper and quality stationery and a wide range of loose and bagged artisan teas.

➕ C4 ✉ 3232 P Street NW ☎ 202/333–9141 🕐 Tue–Sat 10–5, Sun 12–4

KIEHL'S

www.kiehls.com

Kiehl's has had a growing following for its skincare products since 1851.

➕ D4 ✉ 3110 M Street NW ☎ 202/333–5101 🕐 Mon–Sat 10–7, Sun 12–6

THE OLD PRINT GALLERY

www.oldprintgallery.com

This gallery stocks antique prints as old as America itself, as well as an impressive collection of *New Yorker* covers.

➕ C4 ✉ 1220 31st Street NW ☎ 202/965–1818 🕐 Tue–Sat 10–5.20

PAPER SOURCE

www.paper-source.com

This two-floor paper store stocks cute cards, fine stationery and book-binding kits.

➕ D4 ✉ 3019 M Street NW ☎ 202/298–5545 🕐 Mon–Sat 10–9, Sun 11–7

URBAN CHIC

www.urbanchiconline.com

Urban Chic features wearable trends and classics from designers that include Diane von Furstenberg and Catherine Malandrino.

➕ C3 ✉ 1626 Wisconsin Avenue NW ☎ 202/338–5398 🕐 Mon–Sat 10–7, Sun 12–6

SECRET ALLEY

Down a cobblestone side street is Georgetown's design district, Cady's Alley, with its high-end home furnishing and fashion designers complementing the local antiques stores. The historic shops open up onto a quaint courtyard where Leopold's Kafe and Konditorei (▷ 80) offers delicious Austrian-inspired gastronomic delights.

Entertainment and Nightlife

51ST STATE TAVERN

www.51ststatetavern.com

A straight-up pub decorated in vintage Guinness ads, 51st State draws regulars with its TVs tuned to sports and chilled drafts.

➕ D4 ✉ 2512 L Street NW ☎ 202/625–2444 ◉ Mon–Thu 4pm–2am, Fri–Sat 4pm–3am, Sun 1pm–2am 🚇 Foggy Bottom

BIRRERIA PARADISO

www.eatyourpizza.com

Downstairs from Pizzeria Paradiso (▷ 80), this temple of beer has 16 of the world's finest varieties on tap and 80 in bottles.

➕ C4 ✉ 3282 M Street NW ☎ 202/337–1245 ◉ Mon–Tue 11.30–10, Wed–Thu 11.30–11, Fri–Sat 11.30am–midnight, Sun 12–10 🚇 Dupont Circle

BLUES ALLEY

www.bluesalley.com

A legendary jazz club, made famous by Dizzy Gillespie, Charlie Byrd and the like, Blues Alley now pulls top national acts.

➕ C4 ✉ Rear 1073 Wisconsin Avenue NW ☎ 202/337–4141 ◉ Daily 6pm–12.30am 🚇 Farragut West, then bus 32 or 36

CLYDE'S

www.clydes.com/georgetown

Clyde's is decked out in dark-wood paneling, and has genuine bartenders and a solid menu.

➕ C4 ✉ 3236 M Street NW ☎ 202/333–9180 ◉ Mon–Thu 11am–midnight, Fri 11am–1am, Sat 10am–1am, Sun 9am–midnight

DEGREES BISTRO

www.ritzcarlton.com

This elegant watering hole draws well-dressed patrons with its sleek black slate bar.

➕ C4 ✉ Ritz-Carlton Hotel, 3100 South Street NW ☎ 202/912–4100 ◉ Daily breakfast, lunch, dinner

J PAUL'S

www.jpaulsdc.com

A popular watering hole in an historical building. Students and tourists rub shoulders with politicians and journalists.

➕ C4 ✉ 3218 M Street NW ☎ 202/333–3450 ◉ Mon–Thu 11.30am–2am, Fri 11.30am–3am, Sat 10.30am–3am, Sun 10.30am–2am

JOHN F. KENNEDY CENTER

DC's top spot for renowned performers (▷ 74).

MARTIN'S TAVERN

www.martinstavern.com

This distinguished but unpretentious saloon was a favorite of a young JFK and Jackie. Dark leather booths are named after the famous presidential faces who have dined here.

➕ C4 ✉ 1264 Wisconsin Avenue NW ☎ 202/333–7370 ◉ Mon–Thu 11am–1.30am, Fri 11am–2.30am, Sat 9am–2.30am, Sun 8am–1.30am

MATÉ

www.matedc.com

This chic lounge offers sushi and ceviche, as well as specialty cocktails.

➕ C5 ✉ 3101 K Street NW ☎ 202/333–2006 ◉ Sun–Thu 4pm–12.30am, Fri–Sat 5pm–1am

SEQUOIA

www.arkrestaurants.com/sequoia

On the waterfront with a lovely view over the river.

➕ D5 ✉ 3000 K Street NW ☎ 202/944–4200 ◉ Daily lunch, dinner

THOMPSON BOAT CENTER

www.thompsonboatcenter.com

Canoes, rowing shells, kayaks and bikes for rent.

➕ D5 ✉ 2900 Virginia Avenue NW ☎ 202/333–9543 ◉ Rentals: daily 8–5; closed Nov–early Mar 🚇 Foggy Bottom

THE TOMBS

www.tombs.com

This subterranean bar, adorned with vintage crew prints and oars, is popular among students.

➕ B4 ✉ 1226 36th Street NW ☎ 202/337–6668 ◉ Mon–Thu 11.30am–1.30am, Fri 11.30am–2.30am, Sat 11am–2.30am, Sun 9.30am–1.30am

HALF-PRICE TICKETS

TICKETplace (www.ticketplace.org) offers same-day half-price tickets (online only) to a variety of shows around town. There is a variable service charge. Many theaters also sell discounted preview week or last-minute tickets.

Restaurants

PRICES	
Prices are approximate, based on a 3-course meal for one person.	
$$$	over $50
$$	$30–$50
$	under $30

1789 ($$$)

www.1789restaurant.com
In a renovated Federal-style town house with a large fireplace, 1789 specializes in innovatively prepared game and seafood.
🚩 B4 ✉ 1226 36th Street NW ☎ 202/965–1789 🕐 Mon–Thu 6–10, Fri 6–11, Sat 5.30–11, Sun 5.30–10 🚇 Foggy Bottom, then bus 32 or 38B

BISTRO FRANÇAIS ($$$)

www.bistrofrancaisdc.com
Delicious classic French cuisine at reaonable prices in this award-winning restaurant. With crisp, white tablecloths and vintage French posters, you could almost be in Paris. There's also an extensive wine list.
🚩 C4 ✉ 3124 M Street NW ☎ 202/338–3830 🕐 Sun–Thu 11am–3am, Fri–Sat 11am–4am 🚇 Foggy Bottom–GWU

CAFÉ BONAPARTE ($–$$)

www.cafebonaparte.com
The draw at this charming intimate bistro with sidewalk seating, dark red walls and a silver ceiling is the delicious sweet and savory crepes. It bills itself as "the quintessential European café, creperie, coffeeshop and bar."
🚩 C4 ✉ 1522 Wisconsin Avenue NW ☎ 202/333–8830 🕐 Daily 11–3.30, 5.30–10; closed Sun evening

DEAN AND DELUCA ($)

www.deandeluca.com
A picnicker's paradise, this grocer carries, among other things, the finest fruit, chocolate and cheese and a dazzling array of gourmet prepared foods.
🚩 C4 ✉ 3276 M Street NW ☎ 202/342–2500 🕐 Mon–Sat 8am–9pm, Sun 8–8

LEOPOLD'S KAFE AND KONDITOREI ($$$)

www.kafeleopolds.com
This Austrian café offers dishes ranging from veal schnitzel to a delicious selection of salads. Leopold's also has a huge pastry selection. Everything is served à la carte.

🚩 C4 ✉ 3315 M Street NW ☎ 202/965–6005 🕐 Daily breakfast, lunch, dinner

MISS SAIGON ($–$$)

www.ms-saigonus.com
An extensive menu of traditional Vietnamese dishes is expertly prepared at this popular, atmospheric restaurant.
🚩 D4 ✉ 3057 M Street NW ☎ 202/333–5545 🕐 Sun–Thu 11.30–10.30, Fri–Sat 11.30–11 🚇 Foggy Bottom, then 15-min walk

NICK'S RIVERSIDE GRILL ($$)

www.nicksriversidegrill.com
Family-run restaurant in Georgetown's Washington Harbour. The sleek, contemporary restaurant and outdoor terrace have views river over the Potomac River.
🚩 D5 ✉ 3050 K Street NW ☎ 202/342–3535 🕐 Sun–Thu 11.30am–1.30am, Fri–Sat 11.30am–2.30am 🚇 Foggy Bottom, then 15-min walk

PIZZERIA PARADISO ($)

www.eatyourpizza.com
The stone, wood-burning oven is the heart of this restaurant, which pumps out the best Neapolitan pizza in town. There are 16 different beers on tap and a good selection of wines. Also available for carryout.
🚩 C4 ✉ 3282 M Street NW ☎ 202/337–1245 🕐 Mon–Tue 11.30–10, Wed–Thu 11.30–11, Fri–Sat 11.30am–midnight, Sun 12–10

Mostly residential, Northwest Washington is home to shady streets and most of DC's embassies and mansions. With more than its fair share of restaurants and bars, it's also a popular nighttime destination.

Northwest Washington

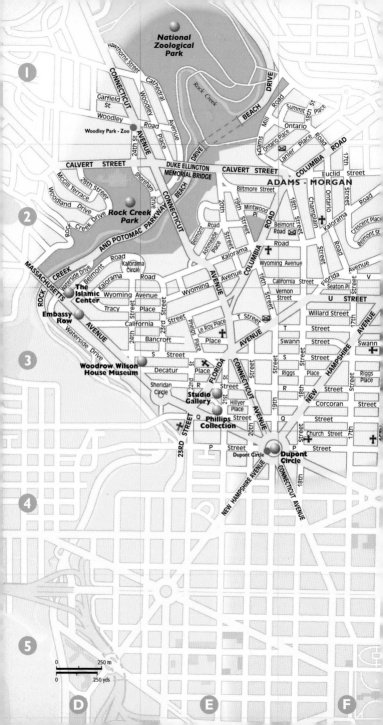

National Zoological Park

Exploring panda (left) and a male lion (right) at the National Zoological Park

THE BASICS

www.nationalzoo.si.edu

🚇 E1

✉ 3001 Connecticut Avenue NW

☎ 202/633–4888

🕐 Grounds: Apr–Oct daily 6am–8pm; Nov–Mar 6–6. Animal buildings: Apr–Oct daily 10–6; Nov–Mar 10–4.30

♿ Free. Parking charge

👍 Excellent

🍴 Snack bars, cafés

Ⓜ Woodley Park–Zoo

HIGHLIGHTS

● Bao Bao, the Panda
● Amazonia
● Orangutans on the "O line"
● Bird House
● Elephants
● Lions, tigers and cheetahs
● Kids' Farm
● Weekend walking tours

Founded in 1889, this 163-acre (66ha) park, one of America's finest zoos, is home to more than 2,000 animals from over 400 species. Come here to see seals jump, monkeys swing and crocs swim.

Before elephants and donkeys A national zoo was the vision of William Hornaday, who was a taxidermist at the Smithsonian. Hornaday opened a trial zoo, packed with animals including bears and bison, right outside the Smithsonian Castle on the Mall. Not surprisingly, Congress soon approved a site a little farther away in Rock Creek Park, which the zoo still calls home. Plans for the spot were drawn up by Hornaday and Frederick Law Olmsted, Jr., son of the designer of Central Park in New York. When Hornaday was not chosen as the first director of the zoo, he left and founded the Bronx Zoo.

America's park More than two million visitors a year come to see the zoo's massive collection of flora and fauna. At the moment, the zoo's most popular inhabitant is the baby panda Bao Bao, who was born in August 2013 to Mei Xiang and Tian Tian, who replaced the famous Ling-Ling and Hsing-Hsing that were gifts from China following President Nixon's historic visit in 1972. Visitors also come to see the big cats, the "O line," which allows orangutans to swing freely, Amazonia and the Reptile Discovery Center. Bison were introduced to celebrate the zoo's 125th anniversary in 2014.

The former home of Duncan Phillips, housing the Phillips Collection, a gallery of modern art

Phillips Collection

This collection in the former house of Duncan Phillips was one of America's first museums of modern art and is still internationally renowned for its collection of Impressionist and Post-Impressionist paintings.

Duncan Phillips In 1918, after the premature death of his father and brother, Phillips established a gallery in their honor in a room of his Georgian revival home. Over the years, Phillips and his wife Marjorie, a painter, continued to buy art with a keen eye. Phillips believed strongly in an art lineage—that artists were clearly influenced by their predecessors as they were in turn by those who came before them. The size of his collection grew to more than 3,000 works, including some selections that were risky at the time—Georgia O'Keeffe, Mark Rothko and Pierre Bonnard. They also bought Auguste Renior's *Luncheon of the Boating Party* for a record price of $125,000. In 1930, Phillips moved out and the collection took over. Phillips continued to direct the gallery until his death in 1966.

Current collection A major renovation project added a new building, increasing the gallery's exhibition space, as well as an auditorium. The permanent collection contains works by Piet Mondrian, Paul Klee, Pablo Picasso, Monet, Degas, Matisse, van Gogh, Cézanne and many well-known American artists. The gallery also continues to add to the collection.

THE BASICS

www.phillipscollection.org

✚ E3

✉ 1600 21st Street NW

☎ 202/387-2151

🕐 Tue–Sat 10–5 (Thu until 8.30), Sun 12–7. Closed public hols

💲 Permanent collection: free weekdays, expensive Sat–Sun. Expensive for temporary exhibitions

♿ Excellent

🍴 Café

Ⓜ Dupont Circle

❓ Tue–Fri short tours noon, 15-min talk on different works of art. Concerts in the Music Room Sep–May Sun 4pm

HIGHLIGHTS

● *Luncheon of the Boating Party*, Auguste Renoir
● *The Way to the Citadel*, Paul Klee
● *Repentant St. Peter*, El Greco
● *Entrance to the Public Garden at Arles*, Vincent van Gogh
● *Dancers at the Barre*, Edgar Degas
● *The Terrace*, Pierre Bonnard

Rock Creek Park

TOP
25

Rock Creek Park in fall (left); Rock Creek (right)

THE BASICS

www.nps.gov/rocr

D2

✉ Nature Center, 5200 Glover Road NW

☎ 202/895–6000; Nature Center 202/895–6070

🕐 Nature Center: Wed–Sun 9–5. Grounds: daylight hours

👋 Free

🚇 Woodley Park–Zoo

HIGHLIGHTS

● Rock Creek Parkway
● Running and biking trails
● Carter Barron Amphitheater
● Nature Center and Planetarium
● Peirce Mill
● The Old Stone House
● Extensive hiking trails

A geological rift that slices through northwest DC, Rock Creek Park is one of the few metropolitan parks to be shaped mainly by its geology, not the work of man. It's a popular park among Washingtonians.

Park of presidents In 1890, President Benjamin Harrison (1833–1901) signed a bill establishing Rock Creek Park as one of the first national parks. The area, over 1,700 acres (687ha), was acquired for a little more than $1 million. While in office, President Theodore Roosevelt, an avid naturalist, would often spend his afternoons hiking in unmarked sections of the park with the French Ambassador, making sure to return after dark so that his appearance "would scandalize no one." Rock Creek Parkway, on the National Registry of Historic Places, was built from 1923 to 1936. During his presidency, Woodrow Wilson would have his driver drop him off in the park with the woman he was courting and then pick them up farther down the road.

Playground of Washingtonians At twice the size of Central Park, Rock Creek Park has enough room for everyone. A paved bike trail leads from the Lincoln Memorial all the way to Maryland, and Beach Drive north of Military Road is closed to motor traffic on the weekends during the day. The park is full of hiking trails and picnic areas, as well as a golf course, tennis courts and horse center.

Washington National Cathedral

The soaring Gothic cathedral has long served as the epicenter of the nation's faith in times of celebration, crisis and sorrow. Its official name is the Cathedral Church of Saint Peter and Saint Paul in the City and Diocese of Washington, but everyone knows it as the National Cathedral.

Presidential past Three US presidents have had their state funeral here: Dwight Eisenhower, Ronald Reagan and Gerald Ford. Several others were honored with prayer or memorial services after their deaths, including John F. Kennedy, Franklin D. Roosevelt, Calvin Coolidge and Harry S. Truman. Fittingly, several presidential inauguration prayer services have also been held here.

Solid foundation The first foundation stone—made of Indiana limestone—was laid in 1907, and the last wasn't set in place until 83 years later, in 1990. Four architects and thousands of masons and sculptors, among other workers, labored to create the majestic Gothic structure, whose tallest tower reaches 300ft (90m) into the sky. In 2011, the cathedral sustained major damage when a 5.8 magnitude earthquake shook the city and the surrounding area. Stones on several pinnacles broke off, gargoyles and other carvings were damaged, and falling stone punched a hole in the roof. The cathedral was closed for several months after the earthquake and repairs, which were still going on in 2015, have been estimated at $26 million.

THE BASICS

www.cathedral.org

✚ B1

✉ 3101 Wisconsin Avenue NW

☎ 202/537–6200

🕐 Mon–Fri 10–5.30, Sat 10–4.30 (Sun services 8–5)

💷 Expensive

🚇 Dupont Circle, then N2, N3, N4 or N6 bus

❓ Tours 10–11.15, 1–3.30; Mon and Wed 12.30 organ demonstrations

HIGHLIGHTS

● Exterior gargoyles
● Bell tower with two sets of bells (53-bell carillon and 10-bell peal)
● Pulpit carved from stones from Canterbury Cathedral
● The Great Organ, installed in 1938
● Pilgrim Observation Gallery
● Sculpture of Darth Vader on top of northwest tower (binoculars required)

More to See

AFRICAN-AMERICAN CIVIL WAR MEMORIAL AND MUSEUM

www.afroamcivilwar.org

This museum tells the story of the 209,145 African-Americans who fought to abolish slavery in the American Civil War. Edward Hamilton's bronze memorial, two blocks east, was dedicated in 1998. ✚ H3 ✉ 1925 Vermont Avenue NW ☎ 202/667-2667 🕐 Museum Tue–Fri 10–6.30, Sat 10–4, Sun 12–4; Memorial 24 hours 🚇 U Street/African-American Civil War Memorial/Cardozo ✋ Free

BISHOP'S GARDEN

Built around European ruins and a statue of the Prodigal Son, this is a gem of a garden at Washington National Cathedral. ✚ B1 ✉ Wisconsin and Massachusetts Avenues NW ☎ 202/537-2937 🕐 Daily dawn–dusk 🚇 Dupont Circle, then N2, N3, N4 or N6 bus ✋ Free

DUPONT CIRCLE

In warmer months, the grassy areas in the center of the Circle team with people. Home to the rich and famous during the early 20th century, Dupont is now home to a younger (but still rich) crowd and is the focus of the city's gay community. ✚ E4 🚇 Dupont Circle

EDWARD KENNEDY "DUKE" ELLINGTON RESIDENCE

Though born at 1217 22nd Street NW, "Duke" Ellington (1899–1974) grew up on this street and took piano lessons nearby. ✚ G3 ✉ 1805–1816 13th Street NW 🕐 Not open to public 🚇 U Street/African-American Civil War Memorial/Cardozo

EMBASSY ROW

Many of the capital's most beautiful embassies line Massachusetts Avenue north of Dupont Circle. ✚ D3 🚇 Dupont Circle

THE ISLAMIC CENTER

www.theislamiccenter.com

From this mosque, built in 1957, calls to the faithful emanate from a 162ft (49m) minaret. The inside is adorned with Persian carpets, ebony and ivory carvings, stained glass and mosaics. ✚ D3 ✉ 2551 Massachusetts Avenue NW ☎ 202/332-8343 🕐 Cultural Center: daily 10–5; mosque: between prayer times 🚇 Dupont Circle

STUDIO GALLERY

www.studiogallerydc.com

Artists in the DC area contribute to the ever-changing exhibitions of contemporary art showcased here. ✚ E3 ✉ 2108 R Street NW ☎ 202/232-8734 🕐 Wed–Fri 1pm–6pm, Sat 11–6 🚇 Dupont Circle

U STREET

U Street was a mecca for jazz musicians and is now experiencing revival and one of the fastest growth rates in the city. ✚ G3 ✉ U Street between 10th and 15th streets 🚇 U Street/African-American Civil War Memorial/Cardozo

WOODROW WILSON HOUSE MUSEUM

www.woodrowwilsonhouse.org

Woodrow Wilson lived here from 1921 until his death in 1924. ✚ D3 ✉ 2340 S Street ☎ 202/387-4062 🕐 Tue–Sun 10–4 🚇 Dupont Circle ✋ Expensive

Cosmopolitan Washington

Dupont's tree-shaded streets and Circle offer a glimpse of both young, hip DC and elegant, old-fashioned architecture.

DISTANCE: 2.5 miles (4km) **ALLOW:** 1 hour 30 minutes

START

DUPONT CIRCLE (▷ 88)
⊞ E4 Ⓜ Dupont Circle

END

DUPONT CIRCLE (▷ 88)
⊞ E4 Ⓜ Dupont Circle

❶ Begin at Dupont Circle Metro's Q Street exit. Go east on Q past Thomas F. Schneider's town houses (1889–92) and the Cairo Apartments (1894).

❷ Turn right on 17th Street, a bustling strip in the warmer months. Take another right on Church Street, which passes some lovely Dupont town houses. Turn left on 18th Street and then right on P Street.

❸ Before you cross over into the Circle, look right to check out the Patterson House, where President Coolidge lived while the White House was being renovated. Many photos of Charles Lindbergh show him waving from this balcony.

❹ Pass into the Circle with the Dupont Memorial Fountain, designed by Lincoln Memorial sculptor Daniel French. Head southwest (roughly left) on New Hampshire Avenue to 1307, the "Brewmaster's Castle."

❽ Turn left onto Decatur Place, left onto Florida Avenue and continue to Connecticut Avenue; Dupont Circle Metro is down the hill.

❼ Past Sheridan Circle, turn right on S Street, which runs along a hilltop park. Walk down the Decatur stairs on your right.

❻ On Massachusetts you will pass the Phillips Collection (▷ 85) and the Anderson House, home of the Society of the Cincinnati.

❺ Turn right onto 20th, then left onto Massachusetts. On the left is the Walsh Mansion, purchased in 1951 by Indonesia for a tenth of the $3 million it cost to build in 1903.

NORTHWEST WASHINGTON WALK

Shopping

BEADAZZLED
www.beadazzled.net
A playground for those who make their own jewelry, this store stocks a massive collection of beads, tools and books.
🔲 E3 ✉ 1507 Connecticut Avenue NW ☎ 202/265–2323 🕐 Mon–Sat 10–8, Sun 11–6 🚇 Dupont Circle

BETSY FISHER
www.betsyfisher.com
Carrying designers like Nanette Lapore and Diane von Furstenberg, along with a few local designers, Betsy Fisher draws women young, old and in between.
🔲 F4 ✉ 1224 Connecticut Avenue NW ☎ 202/785–1975 🕐 Mon–Wed 10–7, Thu–Fri 10–8, Sat 10–6, Sun 12–4 🚇 Dupont Circle

BLUE MERCURY
www.bluemercury.com
Aside from its hard-to-match selection of hair- and skin-care products, Blue Mercury also provides Diptyque candles and a number of spa treatments.
🔲 E3 ✉ 1619 Connecticut Avenue NW ☎ 202/462–1300 🕐 Mon–Sat 10–8, Sun 11–6 🚇 Dupont Circle

CALVERT WOODLEY LIQUORS
www.calvertwoodley.com
In business for more than two decades, Calvert Woodley stocks DC's largest selection of wine as well as a range of fantastic cheese.
🔲 D1 ✉ 4339 Connecticut Avenue NW ☎ 202/966–4400 🕐 Mon–Fri 10–8.30, Sat 9.30–8.30 🚇 Woodley Park–Zoo

CLAUDE TAYLOR PHOTOGRAPHY
www.travelphotography.net
Beautiful, evocative photographic prints from around the world.
🔲 E3 ✉ 1627 Connecticut Avenue NW ☎ 202/518–4000 🕐 Mon–Sat 10–9, Sun 10–8 🚇 Dupont Circle

COFFEE AND THE WORKS
This narrow store is filled with high-end kitchenware, and a good selection of tea and coffee.
🔲 E3 ✉ 1627 Connecticut Avenue NW ☎ 202/483–8050 🕐 Daily 10.30–9.30 🚇 Dupont Circle

---

SPECIAL-INTEREST TOMES

Specialist books can be located at the headquarters of the hundreds of professional associations, think tanks and foundations in Washington—the Brookings Institution, the Carnegie Endowment for International Peace, the Freedom Forum, the American Alliance of Museums, the American Institute of Architects, and even the American Society of Association Executives. For particular subject interests you'll find plenty of choice.

CROOKED BEAT RECORDS
www.crookedbeat.com
This Adams Morgan shop is the place to find new and used LPs covering all genres from punk to reggae and soul.
🔲 F2 ✉ 2116 18th Street NW ☎ 202/483–2328 🕐 Mon 1.30pm–8pm, Tue–Sat 12–9, Sun 12–7 🚇 Dupont Circle

GOOD WOOD
www.goodwooddc.com
This friendly U Street shop carries high-quality, reasonably priced furniture, housewares and vintage jewelry.
🔲 G3 ✉ 1428 U Street NW ☎ 202/986–3640 🕐 Mon–Sat 12–7, Sun 12–5 🚇 U Street/African-American Civil War Memorial/Cardozo

HEMPHILL FINE ARTS
www.hemphillfinearts.com
In up-and-coming Logan Circle, this large gallery stocks an impressive array of American artists.
🔲 G4 ✉ 1515 14th Street NW, 3rd floor ☎ 202/234–5601 🕐 Thu–Sat 10–5 🚇 U Street/African-American Civil War Memorial/Cardozo

KRAMERBOOKS AND AFTERWORDS CAFÉ
www.kramers.com
This bookstore/bar/brunch spot/late-night hangout is always buzzing with activity—from those browsing for their next read among the well-picked selection to those looking for their next date.

E3 ✉ 1517 Connecticut Avenue NW ☎ 202/387–3825 ⏰ Sun–Thu 7.30am–1am, Fri–Sat 7.30am–4am 🚇 Dupont Circle

MEEPS FASHIONETTE

www.meepsdc.com
Stocks well-priced men's and women's vintage clothing, along with a "local focus" section.

F3 ✉ 2104 18th Street NW ☎ 202/265–6546 ⏰ Mon–Wed 12–7, Thu–Fri 12–8, Sat 11–8, Sun 11–6 🚇 U Street/African-American Civil War Memorial/Cardozo

MISS PIXIE'S

www.misspixies.com
Stocked with low-price antiques and vintage home furnishings, Miss Pixie's is popular among a young, hip crowd.

G2 ✉ 1626 14th Street NW ☎ 202/232-8171 ⏰ Daily 12–7 🚇 U Street/African-American Civil War Memorial/Cardozo

PROPER TOPPER

www.propertopper.com
Fashionable headwear is the main draw, but also come for myriad accessories and home decor.

F4 ✉ 1350 Connecticut Avenue NW ✉ 202/842-3055 ⏰ Mon–Fri 10–8, Sat 10–7, Sun 12–6 🚇 Dupont Circle

RIZIK BROTHERS

www.riziks.com
From evening wear through bridal wear to casual day clothes and coats and jackets, Rizik's

has been around for nearly a century and continues to please. There's a good range of accessories, too.

F4 ✉ 1100 Connecticut Avenue NW ✉ 202/223-4050 ⏰ Mon–Sat 9–6 (Thu till 8) 🚇 Farragut North

SECONDI

www.secondi.com
Washington's top stop for secondhand clothes, Secondi is no thrift store—despite the prices. Brands include Marc Jacobs, Prada and Louis Vuitton.

E3 ✉ 1702 Connecticut Avenue NW, 2nd floor ☎ 202/667–1122 ⏰ Mon–Tue 11–6, Wed–Fri 11–7, Sat 11–6, Sun 1–5 🚇 Dupont Circle

SECOND STORY BOOKS

www.secondstorybooks.com
If used books are your passion, start here. If you don't find your treasure, it may be in Second Story's warehouse.

E4 ✉ 2000 P Street NW ☎ 202/659–8884 ⏰ Daily 10–10 🚇 Dupont Circle

SMASH RECORDS

www.smashrecords.com
Vinyl, vintage clothes and

TREASURE HUNTING

Georgetown, Adams-Morgan, Dupont Circle and the 7th Street art corridor are abundantly supplied with galleries, boutiques and specialist stores.

a cool vibe. A knowledge-able staff are on hand to help you find your way around everything from hip-hop to hard core punk, disco to dub step.

F2 ✉ 2314 18th Street NW, 2nd floor ☎ 202/387–6274 ⏰ Mon–Thu 12–9, Fri–Sat 12–9.30, Sun 12–7 🚇 U Street/African-American Civil War Memorial/Cardozo

TABLETOP

www.tabletopdc.com
Sleek retro housewares are the calling card of this location. Items are well designed and priced as such, but be sure not to forget the bargain area in the back.

E3 ✉ 1608 20th Street NW ☎ 202/387–7117 ⏰ Mon–Sat 12–8, Sun 10–6 🚇 Dupont Circle

THOMAS PINK

www.thomaspink.com
High-end, yet inviting, this branch of the English shirtmaker caters to both men and women.

F4 ✉ 1127 Connecticut Avenue NW ☎ 202/223-5390 ⏰ Mon–Fri 10–7 (Thu till 8), Sat 10–6, Sun 12–5 🚇 Farragut North

VIOLET BOUTIQUE

www.violetdc.com
A collection of fun, trendy and stylish clothes and accessories for all occasions at great prices.

F2 ✉ 439 18th Street NW ☎ 202/621–9225 ⏰ Tue–Fri 12–8, Sat 11–8, Sun 11–6 🚇 U Street/African-American Civil War Memorial/Cardozo

NORTHWEST WASHINGTON SHOPPING

Entertainment and Nightlife

9:30 CLUB

www.930.com

See the most popular non-stadium acts take the stage at this well-designed club.

⊞ H2 ✉ 815 V Street NW ☎ 202/265–0930 🕐 Hours vary, check website 🚇 U Street/African-American Civil War Memorial/Cardozo

BOHEMIAN CAVERNS

The club has showcased performers such as Duke Ellington, and continues to attract jazz muscians.

⊞ G3 ✉ 2001 11th Street NW ☎ 202/299–0800 🕐 Mon–Thu 7pm–midnight, Fri–Sat 7.30pm–2am, Sun 6pm–midnight 🚇 U Street/African-American Civil War Memorial/Cardozo

CAFÉ CITRON

Live Latin music and well-priced mojitos keep this spot hot.

⊞ F4 ✉ 1343 Connecticut Avenue NW ☎ 202/530–8844 🕐 Mon–Thu 4pm–2am, Fri–Sat 4pm–3am 🚇 Dupont Circle

CHI-CHA LOUNGE

www.chichaloungedc.com

A plush lounge filled with sofas and young professionals, Chi-Cha offers live Latin jazz, Andean tapas, a tasty namesake drink and hookahs.

⊞ F3 ✉ 1624 U Street NW ☎ 202/234–8400 🕐 Sun–Thu 5pm–11.30pm, Fri–Sat 5pm–1.30am 🚇 U Street/African-American Civil War Memorial/Cardozo, Dupont Circle

EIGHTEENTH STREET LOUNGE (ESL)

www.eighteenthstreetlounge.com

This multilevel house party is popular among Washington's most chic. You'll need to dress well.

⊞ F4 ✉ 1212 18th Street NW ☎ 202/696–0210 🕐 Tue–Thu 5.30pm–2am, Fri 5.30pm–3am, Sat 9.30pm–3am, Sun 9.30pm–2am. No admittance 30 min before closing; cover charge 🚇 Dupont Circle

MARVIN

www.marvindc.com

Eighteenth Street Lounge's more accessible sister.

⊞ G3 ✉ 2007 14th Street NW ☎ 202/797–7171 🕐 Sun–Thu 5pm–2am, Fri–Sat 5pm–3am 🚇 U Street/African-American Civil War Memorial/Cardozo

ADAMS-MORGAN

By far the liveliest and most eclectic nightlife scene in town is in Adams-Morgan. The strip, wall-to-wall bars and restaurants on 18th Street NW from Kalorama Road to Columbia Avenue and then spilling east and west, has something for everyone, such as Bourbon, a whisky bar; Habana Village with salsa dancing and mojitos; Madam's Organ with nightly live music; Rumba Cafe with live Latin music; and Club Timehri, a Caribbean nightclub.

SALOON

The Saloon prohibits standing and ordering martinis, but regulars find the select beer list and the conversation inviting.

⊞ E3 ✉ 1205 U Street NW ☎ 202/462–2640 🕐 Tue–Thu 11am–1am, Fri 11am–2am, Sat 2pm–2am 🚇 U Street/African-American Civil War Memorial/Cardozo

STUDIO THEATRE

www.studiotheatre.org

This independent company produces an eclectic season of classic and offbeat plays.

⊞ G4 ✉ 1501 14th Street NW ☎ 202/332–3300 🚇 Dupont Circle

TABARD INN

www.tabardinn.com

This hotel's warm sitting room has sofas, wood paneling, a fireplace and jazz on Sunday, Monday and Tuesday nights.

⊞ F4 ✉ 1739 N Street NW ☎ 202/785–1277 🕐 Mon–Fri 11.30am–last call, Sat–Sun 10.30am–last call 🚇 Dupont Circle

U STREET MUSIC HALL

www.ustreetmusichall.com

A basement club and live music venue. The 500-person limit keeps it intimate, while one of the city's best sound systems keeps it loud.

⊞ G3 ✉ 1115 U Street NW ☎ 202/588-1889 🕐 Hours vary, check website 🚇 U Street/African-American Civil War Memorial/Cardozo

Restaurants

PRICES

Prices are approximate, based on a 3-course meal for one person.

$$$ over $50
$$ $30–$50
$ under $30

AMSTERDAM FALAFELSHOP ($)

www.falafelshop.com
Falafel and fries may be the only thing on the menu here, but dozens of fresh toppings—sauces, salads and pickles—make the difference.
⊞ F2 ✉ 2425 18th Street NW ☎ 202/234-1969
◉ Daily 11am–very late
⊜ Woodley Park-Zoo

BEN'S CHILI BOWL ($)

www.benschilibowl.com
This U Street institution sells burgers, hot dogs and fries to a late-night crowd.
⊞ G3 ✉ 1213 U Street NW ☎ 202/667-0909 ◉ Mon–Sat breakfast, lunch, dinner, late night; Sun lunch, dinner
⊜ U Street

BRIXTON ($)

www.brixtondc.com
British-style pub with regular happy hours, serving pub grub with an interesting twist. The Lodge Bar has brick-lined walls and welcoming fireplace and the roof deck has great views over the city.
⊞ H3 ✉ 901 U Street NW ☎ 202/5600-5045 ◉ Mon–Thu 5pm–late, Fri 5pm–3am, Sat 3pm–3am, Sun 3pm–late
⊜ U Street/African-American Civil War Memorial/Cardozo

BUKOM CAFÉ ($)

www.bukomcafe.com
Sunny African pop music, and a spicy West African menu filled with goat and lamb. Open late; live music nightly.
⊞ F2 ✉ 2442 18th Street NW ☎ 202/265-4600
◉ Daily dinner ⊜ Woodley Park-Zoo, then bus 92 or 96

BUSBOYS AND POETS ($–$$)

www.busboysandpoets.com
A hip coffee shop, bookstore, restaurant, art gallery and performance space, Busboys and Poets has quickly become a gathering spot for this neighborhood.
⊞ G3 ✉ 2021 14th Street NW ☎ 202/387-7638

MULTICULTURAL

The city's most multicultural neighborhood is crowded, bustling and filled with ethnic restaurants. A walk along 18th Street leads past: **Bukom Café** and **The Diner** (see main entries this page); **Duken** (Ethiopian ✉ 1114–1118 U Street ☎ 202/667-8735); **Little Fountain Café** (International ✉ 2339 18th Street ☎ 202/462-8100); **Meskerem** (Ethiopian ✉ 2434 18th Street ☎ 202/462-4100); and **Mezè** (▷ 94).

◉ Sun 9am–midnight, Mon–Thu 8am–midnight, Fri 8am–1am, Sat 9am–1am ⊜ U Street/African-American Civil War Memorial/Cardozo

LE DIPLOMATE ($$$)

www.lediplomatedc.com
This popular Parisian-style brasserie is a favored haunt of DC celebrities. Book ahead.
⊞ G3 ✉ 1601 14th Street NW ☎ 202/332-3333
◉ Daily dinner from 5pm, Sat–Sun brunch 9.30–3, aprés-midi 3–5 ⊜ Dupont Circle

HANK'S OYSTER BAR ($$)

www.hanksoysterbar.com
This narrow, lively seafood stop serves up simple, yet skillful, dishes that draw your attention to the finest, high-quality ingredients.
⊞ F3 ✉ 1624 Q Street NW ☎ 202/462-4265 ◉ Daily lunch, dinner ⊜ Dupont Circle

INDIQUE ($$)

www.indique.com
Modern Indian food, creative cocktails and an icy cool setting draw in a sophisticated crowd.
⊞ Off map at D1 ✉ 3512 Connecticut Avenue NW ☎ 202/244-6600 ◉ Mon–Thu dinner, Fri–Sun lunch, dinner ⊜ Cleveland Park

KOMI ($$$)

www.komirestaurant.com
Young chef Johnny Monis draws foodies from all over the city with his basic, yet inspired, dishes

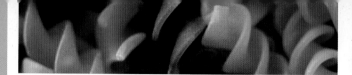

crafted with fantastic ingredients. The cuisine has Greek influences. Reservations essential.
➕ F3 ✉ 1509 17th Street NW ☎ 202/332–9200
🕐 Tue–Sat dinner
🚇 Dupont Circle

LAURIOL PLAZA ($)

www.lauriolplaza.com
Popular among young Hill staff for its open-air top floor and slushy margaritas. The Latin American food isn't too bad, either.
➕ F3 ✉ 1835 18th Street NW ☎ 202/387–0035
🕐 Daily lunch, dinner
🚇 Dupont Circle

LEBANESE TAVERNA ($–$$)

www.lebanesetaverna.com
Specializing in Lebanese *meze*, this popular restaurant is known for its warm hospitality.
➕ E1 ✉ 2641 Connecticut Avenue NW ☎ 202/265–8681 🕐 Daily lunch, dinner
🚇 Woodley Park–Zoo

MEZÈ ($–$$)

www.mezedc.com
This cool Turkish spot churns out tasty *meze* and offers a roomy patio for the warmer months.
➕ F2 ✉ 2437 18th Street ☎ 202/797–0017 🕐 Mon–Thu 4.30pm–1.30am, Fri 4.30pm–2.30am, Sat 10.30am–2.30am, Sun 10.30am–1.30am
🚇 Woodley Park–Zoo

NORA ($$$)

www.noras.com
The nation's first restaurant to be certified as organic, Nora offers a menu of free-range meats and seafood in a dining room beautifully decorated with Amish quilts.
➕ E3 ✉ 2132 Florida Avenue NW ☎ 202/462–5143 🕐 Mon–Sat dinner
🚇 Dupont Circle

RUSSIA HOUSE LOUNGE ($$$)

www.russiahouselounge.com
Russian-European elegance with sumptuous decor in rich colors. Choose from workaday borsch to budget-blowing caviar.
➕ E3 ✉ 1800 Connecticut Avenue NW ☎ 202/234–9322 🕐 Sun–Thu 5pm–10pm, Sat 5pm–11pm
🚇 Dupont Circle

SATELLITE ($)

www.satellitedc.com
Fun California-style diner serving burgers, beer and alcoholic milk shakes.
➕ H3 ✉ 2047 9th Street NW ☎ 202/506–2496
🕐 Mon–Fri 5pm–close, Sat–Sun 11–4 🚇 U Street/African-American Civil War Memorial/Cardozo

---

LATE-NIGHT EATS

There are many places in town that cater to the late-night crowd and they typically serve outstanding nosh. If you've got the munchies late, try The Diner (▷ 93), Kramerbooks and Afterwords Café (▷ 90) or Ben's Chili Bowl (▷ 93).

SUSHI TARO ($$–$$$)

www.sushitaro.com
This sushi powerhouse always has three grades of tuna on hand, along with a large selection of ultrafresh seafood.
➕ F4 ✉ 1503 17th Street NW ☎ 202/462–8999
🕐 Mon–Fri lunch, dinner; Sat dinner 🚇 Dupont Circle

TEAISM ($)

www.teaism.com
This simple teahouse offers an eclectic collection of Asian-inspired dishes and good-value Japanese bento boxes.
➕ E3 ✉ 2009 R Street NW ☎ 202/667–3827 🕐 Daily breakfast, lunch, dinner
🚇 Dupont Circle

THAI CHEF ($)

www.thaichefsushibardc.com
The decor may be plain, but this kitchen has some of the best Thai food in town; also sushi.
➕ E3 ✉ 1712 Connecticut Avenue NW ☎ 202/234–5698 🕐 Daily lunch, dinner
🚇 Dupont Circle

WELL-DRESSED BURRITO ($)

www.thewelldressedburrito.com
This lunch spot has been selling freshly prepared Mexican takeout for nearly 30 years. The "well-dressed," a large, inexpensive burrito, changes daily.
➕ E4 ✉ 1220 19th Street NW ☎ 202/293–0515
🕐 Mon–Fri lunch 🚇 Dupont Circle

Farther Afield

Suburban congressional staff, tired of traveling all the way into the city for food and entertainment, are spending their money at home instead, spurring quick growth in areas just outside the District.

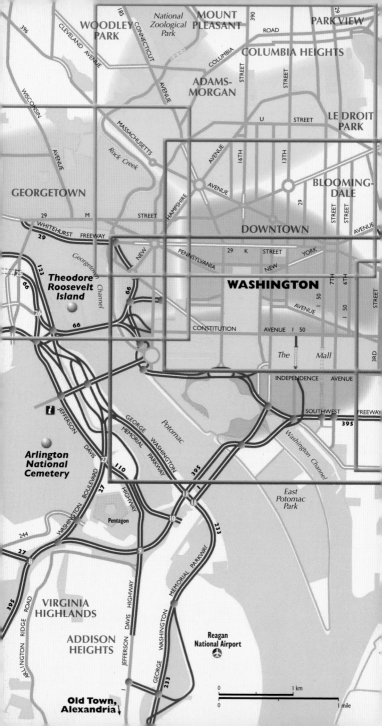

Shrine of the Immaculate Conception

METROPOLIS VIEW

LANGDON

STREET

13TH STREET

212

1

AVENUE

DOBBINS ADDITION

RHODE

ISLAND

EDGEWOOD

50

ECKINGTON

YORK

AVENUE

IVY CITY

ROAD

BLADENSBURG

CAPITOL

NEW

NORTH

FLORIDA

AVENUE

TRINIDAD

National Arboretum

Anacostia Park

MASSACHUSETTS

H STREET

STANTON PARK

AVENUE

MARYLAND

AVENUE

BENNING ROAD

ROSEDALE

CONSTITUTION AVENUE

NORTH CAROLINA AVENUE

CAPITOL HILL

214

INDEPENDENCE AVENUE

STREET

PENNSYLVANIA

AVENUE

SOUTHEAST

CAPITOL

M STREET

FREEWAY

Park

River

Anacostia

Anacostia

FREEWAY

295

ANACOSTIA

MINNESOTA AVENUE

4

SOUTH

Frederick Douglass National Historic Site

Fort Stanton Park

Anacostia Community Museum

GARFIELD HEIGHTS

CAPITOL STREET

295

SUITLAND

PARKWAY

DOUGLASS

Farther Afield

Arlington National Cemetery

HIGHLIGHTS

- Kennedy graves
- Tomb of the Unknowns
- Custis-Lee Mansion
- L'Enfant's grave
- USS *Maine* Memorial
- Shuttle *Challenger* Memorial
- Astronauts Memorial
- Changing of the Guard at the Tomb of the Unknowns

TIP

- Remember that many visit to pay their respects. Dress appropriately and keep an eye on children.

The national cemetery since 1864, Arlington contains the most visited grave in the country, that of John F. Kennedy. Rows and rows of white crosses commemorate the war dead and national heroes with dignity.

Lest we forget Veterans from every American war are interred here on the land of General Robert E. Lee's (1807–70) Arlington House. Those who fought and died before the Civil War were moved here after 1900. Perhaps the most famous soldiers to be buried here are those that have not yet been named. The Tomb of the Unknowns contains remains of a World War I, World War II and Korean War soldier. A soldier from the Vietnam War was disinterred in 1998 after DNA evidence identified him. Sentries

Clockwise from left: Mast of Battleship Maine surrounded by gravestones in Arlington National Cemetery; Changing of the Guard at the Tomb of the Unknowns; the rooftops of the city of Washington, viewed from the hillside of the cemetery; visitors among the graves and blossom-covered trees

from the Third US Infantry guard the tomb 24 hours a day and perform the Changing of the Guard ceremony. Other memorials throughout the cemetery commemorate particular events or groups of people, including those killed in the Pentagon on September 11, 2001, and those aboard the Space Shuttle *Columbia* that crashed in 2003.

White markers and a flame Under an eternal flame, John F. Kennedy lies next to his wife, Jacqueline Bouvier Kennedy Onassis, and two of his children who died in infancy. Nearby lies his brother, Robert, whose grave is marked by a simple white cross and a fountain. The Custis-Lee Mansion sits above the Kennedy graves. Just off the house's west corner lies the grave of Pierre L'Enfant, the city's designer.

THE BASICS

www.arlingtoncemetery. mil

✚ C8

✉ Across Memorial Bridge from Lincoln Memorial

☎ 877/907–8585

🕐 Apr–Sep daily 8–7; Oct–Mar 8–5

💲 Free

♿ Excellent. Visitors with disabilities may board Arlington National Cemetery tour bus free of charge

🚇 Arlington Cemetery

❓ Interpretive tour bus service departs continuously from the Welcome Center. Changing of the Guard: Apr–Sep daily on the half hour; Oct–Mar daily on the hour

Frederick Douglass National Historic Site

TOP 25

The colonial-style exterior of Cedar Hill (left and opposite); inside Frederick Douglass's home (right)

THE BASICS

www.nps.gov/frdo

➕ See map ▷ 97

✉ 1411 W Street SE

☎ 202/426–5961

🕐 Park Apr–Oct daily 9–5; Nov–Mar 9–4.30; tours 9, 12.15, 1.15, 3 and 3.30 (also 4 from Apr–Oct)

🖐 Free

♿ Good

🚇 Anacostia, then B-2 Mt. Rainier bus

🚌 Free weekend Shuttle Anacostia service from Memorial Day–Labor Day

🚗 11th Street Bridge to Martin Luther King Avenue, right on W Street

HIGHLIGHTS

● Frederick Douglass's library
● Portraits of Elizabeth Cady Stanton and Susan B. Anthony
● View of Washington

Built in 1855, the Italianate country house known as Cedar Hill was the last home of abolitionist Frederick Douglass. Decorative arts, libraries and family mementoes provide an intimate look at his life and work.

Slave America's famous abolitionist was born into slavery in Maryland around 1818 and separated from his mother at birth. When Douglass was 12, his master's wife illegally taught him how to read. He escaped to Maryland when he was 20, becoming active in the Massachusetts anti-slavery movement. He wrote an autobiography in 1845, which became so popular that he had to flee to Europe out of fear that his former master would find out and he would be recaptured. There, British friends bought him his freedom, and he lectured widely on anti-slavery topics. When he moved into Cedar Hill, he was the first black resident of Anacostia, breaking the prohibition against "Irish, Negro, mulatto, or persons of African blood."

Viewpoint Cedar Hill, now the Frederick Douglass National Historic Site, occupies the highest point in Anacostia, with a great view of the Anacostia River and the capital. At his rolltop desk in the library, Douglass wrote his autobiography *The Life and Times of Frederick Douglass*. The National Park Service, which manages the site, maintains a visitor center and a bookstore specializing in African-American titles.

More to See

ANACOSTIA COMMUNITY MUSEUM

www.anacostia.si.edu

This Smithsonian museum showcases African-American cultural history.

✚ See map ▷ 97 ✉ 1901 Fort Place SE ☎ 202/633–4820 🕓 Daily 10–5 🚇 Anacostia, then bus W2, W3. Free Shuttle Anacostia service from National Mall weekends Memorial Day–Labor Day ✋ Free

NATIONAL ARBORETUM

www.usna.usda.gov

The Arboretum's 446 acres (180ha) invite driving, biking and hiking. The National Herb Garden, National Bonsai Collection, Azalea Walk and a display of the Capitol's original Corinthian columns are also a draw.

✚ See map ▷ 97 ✉ 3501 New York Avenue NE ☎ 202/245–2726 🕓 Fri–Mon 8–5. Weekend tram tours Apr–Oct 🚇 Stadium-Armory, then bus B2 ✋ Free

OLD TOWN, ALEXANDRIA

A well-preserved colonial port town, Old Town's cobblestone streets are packed with early-American homes and taverns. Along the waterfront, tourists picnic as the boats come in.

✚ See map ▷ 96 ✉ Old Town, Alexandria, VA 🚇 King Street–Old Town

SHRINE OF THE IMMACULATE CONCEPTION

www.nationalshrine.com

The largest church in the Western Hemisphere, this Catholic basilica is renowned for its mosaics and is dedicated to the Virgin Mary.

✚ See map ▷ 97 ✉ 400 Michigan Avenue ☎ 202/526–8300 🕓 Apr–Oct daily 7–7; Nov–Mar 7–6. Tours Mon–Sat 9–3, Sun 1.30–3.30 ✋ Free 🚇 Brookland CUA

THEODORE ROOSEVELT ISLAND

www.nps.gov/this

With miles of walking trails through diverse terrain, this island in the Potomac River is a fitting memorial to the naturalist president. A tall bronze statue of Roosevelt can be found in the center of the island.

✚ C5 🚗 Car access from northbound lane of George Washington Memorial Parkway ☎ 703/289–2500 🕓 Daily 6am–10pm

Hydrangeas in the National Arboretum

The Theodore Roosevelt Monument on Theodore Roosevelt Island

Excursions

FREDERICKSBURG

The 40-block National Historic District in this charming Virginia town comprises the house George Washington (1732–99) bought for his mother, a 1752 plantation, President James Monroe's (1758–1831) law offices, an early apothecary shop and the Georgian Chatham Manor, which overlooks the Rappahannock River.

Two Civil War battles were waged in and around town. You can now visit the battlefields and stroll through the nearby wilderness parks. Antiques and rare-book stores and art galleries line the streets. Start at the well-marked visitor center, which dispenses maps and advice.

THE BASICS

www.visitfred.com
Distance: 50 miles (80km)
Journey Time: 1–2 hours
🚹 706 Caroline Street
☎ 540/373–1776
🕐 Mon–Sat 9–5, Sun 11–5
🚆 Amtrak from Union Station
🚗 South on I-95 to exit 133A and follow signs to visitor center

MOUNT VERNON

George Washington's ancestral Virginia estate is the nation's second-most visited historic house after the White House. Washington worked this plantation's 8,000 acres (3,239ha) before he took control of the Continental Army and returned here for good after his presidency.

Washington supervised the expansion of the main house, most notably the addition of the back porch with a view over the Potomac. The mansion is built of yellow pine, painted multiple times with sand to resemble stone. The ornate interior is furnished with fine arts and memorabilia, and history interpreters provide more information. The outbuildings re-create the spaces of a self-sufficient, 18th-century farm, including the smokehouse and laundry, outside kitchen and slave quarters. Don't miss the view of George and Martha Washington's tomb, and allow time to explore the formal garden and follow the forest trail. The Ladies Association was founded in 1853 to preserve the estate.

THE BASICS

www.mountvernon.org
Distance: 15 miles (24km)
Journey Time: 40 minutes
☎ 703/780–2000
🕐 Mar, Sep–Oct daily 9–5; Apr–Aug 8–5; Nov–Feb 9–4
🚆 Huntington Station, then Fairfax Connector bus
🚗 Take 14th Street Bridge (toward National Airport), then south on George Washington Memorial Parkway
🚢 *Spirit of Mount Vernon* from Pier 4, 6th and Water streets SW (☎ 866/302–2469) Mar–Aug Tue–Sun; Sep–Oct Fri–Sun 💲 Expensive

Shopping

FASHION CENTRE

Macy's and Nordstrom anchor the 170 stores in this Pentagon City mall. An open-air mall across the street houses an array of stores from Ann Taylor Loft to Victoria's Secret.

🔲 Off map at C9 ✉ 1100 S Hayes Street at Army-Navy Drive and I-395 S ☎ 703/415-2400 ⏰ Mon–Sat 10–9.30, Sun 11–6 🚇 Pentagon City

FRIENDSHIP HEIGHTS

These three shopping centers are likely to fill any need. The upscale four-floor Mazza Gallerie and the Chevy Chase Pavilion across the street contain a range of upscale shops including Neiman Marcus at Mazza. The über-chic Collection at Chevy Chase has Louis Vuitton and Cartier.

🔲 Off map at A1 ✉ Wisconsin Avenue at Western Avenue ⏰ Mazza Gallerie: Mon–Fri 10–8, Sat 10–7, Sun 12–6. Chevy Chase Pavilion: Mon–Sat 7am–11pm, Sun 7am–9pm. Collection at Chevy Chase: hours vary 🚇 Friendship Heights

HOUSE OF MUSICAL TRADITIONS

www.hmtrad.com
Musical instruments from lap dulcimers to bagpipes are sold at this well-known location.

🔲 Off map at J1 ✉ 7010 Westmoreland Avenue, Takoma Park, MD ☎ 301/270-9090

⏰ Tue–Sat 11–7, Sun–Mon 11–5 🚇 Takoma

IKEA

www.ikea.com
IKEA offers nearly everything you could want to put in your home.

🔲 Off map at M1 ✉ 10100 Baltimore Avenue, College Park, MD ☎ 301/345-6552 ⏰ Mon–Sat 10–9, Sun 10–8 🚇 College Park

POTOMAC MILLS MALL

One of Virginia's most popular destinations. Bargain shoppers will enjoy Banana Republic and Polo at a discount.

🔲 Off map at A9 ✉ 2700 Potomac Mills Circle, Woodbridge, VA ☎ 703/496-9330 ⏰ Mon–Sat 10–9, Sun 11–6

ROYAL TREATMENT

Political staffers don't shirk from putting in their time at work, but they also know how to be pampered. Want to see partisans reeling from a recent loss or reveling in a clear victory? Head to: Aveda (☎ 202/965-1325), Blue Mercury (▷ 90), Grooming Lounge (▷ 29), or Roche Salon (☎ 202/775-0775). Many hotels, like the upscale Mandarin Oriental (▷ 112), the Ritz-Carlton (▷ 112) and the Willard (▷ 112) also have spas that give the ultimate in superb treatments.

TORPEDO FACTORY ART CENTER

www.torpedofactory.org
Pottery, paintings, jewelry, stained glass and other items by local artists, who work in the studios of this former US Naval torpedo station, are on display.

🔲 Off map at F9 ✉ 105 N Union Street, Alexandria, VA ☎ 703/838-4565 ⏰ Daily 10–6, Thu til 9pm 🚇 King Street, then free trolley Sun–Wed 10am–10.15pm, Thu–Sat 10am–midnight

TOURNEAU

www.tourneau.com
With more than 8,000 styles of watch on offer, there is a timepiece for everyone in this smart emporium.

🔲 Off map at C9 ✉ Pentagon City, 1100 South Hayes Street, Arlington ☎ 703/414-8463 ⏰ Mon–Sat 10–9.30, Sun 11–6 🚇 Pentagon City

TYSONS CORNER

www.tysonscornercenter.com
Tysons Corner Center claims Nordstrom, Bloomingdale's and an AMC theater. Tysons Galleria, across the highway, is a little more upscale, with Saks Fifth Avenue and Chanel.

🔲 Off map at A2 ✉ 1961 Chain Bridge Road, Tysons Corner, VA ☎ 888/289-7667 or 703/ 847-7300 ⏰ Center: Mon–Sat 10–9.30, Sun 11–6. Galleria: Mon–Sat 10–9, Sun 12–6 🚗 I-66 west to Route 7 west, then follow signs 🚇 Tysons Corner

Entertainment and Nightlife

ARENA STAGE

www.arenastage.org
This resident company presents dynamically staged and superbly acted American theater.
➕ H8 ✉ 1101 6th Street SW ☎ 202/488-3300
Ⓜ Waterfront-SEU

BIRCHMERE

www.birchmere.com
One of America's top spots to catch bluegrass and folk. Has hosted the likes of Arlo Guthrie.
➕ Off map at D9
✉ 3701 Mount Vernon Avenue, Alexandria, VA
☎ 703/549-7500
Ⓒ Check website for shows
Ⓜ Pentagon City, then taxi

CONTINENTAL

www.continentalpoollounge.com
This billiards hall is adorned with bright, retro decor and several cozy lounges, perfect for relaxing between games.
➕ B5 ✉ 1911 North Fort Myer Drive, Arlington, VA
☎ 703/465-7675 Ⓒ Mon-Fri 11.30am-2am, Sat-Sun 6pm-2am Ⓜ Rosslyn

THE FILLMORE

www.fillmoresilverspring.com
This opulent venue, with chandeliers and state-of-the-art sound system, dishes up regular well-known national acts. Be prepared to stand.
➕ Off map at H1 ✉ 8656 Colesville Road, Silver Spring, MD ☎ 301/960-9999
Ⓒ Box office Mon-Fri 12-6, Sat 11-4 Ⓜ Silver Spring

PUPPET COMPANY PLAYHOUSE

www.thepuppetco.org
This talented puppet troupe performs to children of all ages.
➕ Off map at A1 ✉ 7300 MacArthur Boulevard, Glen Echo, MD ☎ 301/634-5380
Ⓒ Check website for shows
🚌 29

ROCK AND ROLL HOTEL

www.rockandrollhoteldc.com
A popular live-music venue that plays host to solid indie bands.
➕ M5 ✉ 1353 H Street NE
☎ 202/388-7625 Ⓒ Daily 8pm-late Ⓒ Check website for shows Ⓜ Union Station, then 15-block walk

ROUND HOUSE THEATRE

www.roundhousetheatre.org
The Round House Theatre continues to

POLITICAL PUNCHLINES

Two troupes in town specialize in poking fun at both political parties—Capitol Steps (☎ 703/683-8330), a group of former and current Hill staffers, and Gross National Product (☎ 202/783-7212). Washington Improv Theater (WIT) (☎ 202/315-1318) and ComedySportz (☎ 703/294-5233) tend toward more traditional improv, while DC Improv (☎ 202/296-7008) delivers well-known stand-up acts.

produce an eclectic set of professional plays.
➕ Off map at A1 ✉ 4545 East-West Highway, Bethesda, MD ☎ 240/644-1100
Ⓜ Bethesda

SIGNATURE THEATRE

www.signature-theatre.org
This theater has become renowned for its sharply produced musicals, especially those of Steven Sondheim.
➕ Off map at A9 ✉ 4200 Campbell Avenue, Arlington, VA ☎ 703/820-9771
Ⓜ Pentagon City, then taxi

STRATHMORE

www.strathmore.org
This major music venue has great acoustics. It is now home to the Baltimore Symphony Orchestra and the National Philharmonic.
➕ Off map at A1
✉ 5301 Tuckerman Lane, North Bethesda, MD ☎ 301/581-5100
Ⓜ Grosvenor-Strathmore

WOLF TRAP

www.wolftrap.org
The only National Park devoted to the performing arts, Wolf Trap draws top music acts, dance and musical theater to its outdoor amphitheater. In the colder months, performances take place in the Barns at Wolf Trap.
➕ Off map at A1 ✉ Trap Road, Vienna, VA ☎ 703/255-1900 Ⓜ West Falls Church, then Wolf Trap express bus (every 20 min) for summer performances only

Restaurants

FARTHER AFIELD RESTAURANTS

PRICES

Prices are approximate, based on a 3-course meal for one person.

$$$ over $50
$$ $30–$50
$ under $30

GRANVILLE MOORE'S ($$)

www.granvillemoores.com
Formerly a doctor's office, gastropub Granville Moore's now soothes with Belgian beers and mussels. Nothing is ever reheated or frozen here.
🔆 M5 ✉ 1238 H Street NE
☎ 202/399–2546 🕐 Mon–Fri dinner, Sat–Sun lunch, dinner 🚇 Union Station, then taxi or bus X2

GRAPESEED ($$)

www.grapeseedbistro.com
"Choice" is the word at this bistro/wine bar, where scrumptious dishes and delectable wines are available in small portions for tasting.
🔆 Off map at A1 ✉ 4865 Cordell Avenue, Bethesda, MD ☎ 301/986–9592 🕐 Tue–Fri lunch, Mon–Sat dinner 🚇 Bethesda

INN AT LITTLE WASHINGTON ($$$)

www.theinnatlittle washington.com
An extravagant setting and an over-the-top American meal await the rich and famous who come here to sample Chef Patrick O'Connell's kitchen and savor one of the wines from the 14,000-bottle award-winning cellar.
🔆 Off map at A9 ✉ Main Street and Middle Street, Washington, VA ☎ 540/675–3800 🕐 Daily dinner

PHO 75 ($)

Pho, a Vietnamese noodle dish often eaten at breakfast in Vietnam, is served here in nearly 20 varieties—all of them tasty. Spoons are provided if you're not adept with chopsticks.
🔆 A6 ✉ 1721 Wilson Boulevard, Arlington, VA ☎ 703/525–7355 🕐 Daily 9–8 🚇 Rosslyn

RANGE ($$–$$$)

www.voltrange.com
Award-winning chef Bryan Voltaggio's restaurant draws food enthusiasts who come for the expertly cooked American fare. The bread basket has been called "one of the best in the city."
🔆 Off map at B1 ✉ 5335 Wisconsin Avenue NW (Chevy Chase Pavilion)

PICNIC SPOTS

Washington, a city full of public spaces, offers many great spots for picnicking. Try the grassy expanses in Dupont Circle (▷ 88) or Rock Creek Park (▷ 86), on the Mall, around the Tidal Basin (▷ 36), and at Mount Vernon (▷ 103). If you're short on supplies why not try Dean and Deluca (▷ 80)?

☎ 202/803–8020 🕐 Sun–Thu 11.30–10.30, Fri–Sat 11.30–11 🚇 Friendship Heights

RAY'S THE STEAKS ($$)

www.raysthesteaks.com
This stripped-down and reasonably priced bistro focuses on serving some of the best steaks in town. Reservations recommended.
🔆 A6 ✉ 2300 Wilson Boulevard, Arlington, VA ☎ 703/841–7297 🕐 Daily dinner 🚇 Courthouse

RAY'S TO THE THIRD ($)

Burger connoisseurs highly rate the burgers served here. Ring ahead to make a reservation or be prepared to wait.
🔆 A6 ✉ 1650 Wilson Boulevard, Arlington, VA ☎ 703/841–0001 🕐 Sun–Thu 11–10, Fri–Sat 11–11 🚇 Rosslyn

RESTAURANT EVE ($$$)

www.restauranteve.com
The decor at Cathal Armstrong's restaurant, in an "Eden" theme, sets the stage for what comes next, Modern American cuisine that's truly inspired. Take your pick of several courses from the tasting menus.
🔆 Off map at E9 ✉ 110 South Pitt Street, Alexandria, VA ☎ 703/706–0450 🕐 Bistro: Mon–Fri lunch, dinner; Sat dinner. Tasting menu, dinner only

Washington DC has a range of accommodation options, from bed-and-breakfasts and boutique guesthouses to chain and business-class hotels.

Introduction

Forced to cater to all, from lobbyists oozing money to those in town for the free museums, from bigwigs seeking attention to those flying under the radar—intentionally or not—Washington's rooms suit everyone.

Diplomats at Breakfast

The high-end and business-class hotels tend to be near the halls of power, whether in Georgetown row houses, at the White House or on Capitol Hill. Downtown also has its fair share. There's a good chance that if you stay in one of the pricier digs you'll run into diplomats at breakfast and brush shoulders with heads of state (or their security guards) in the elevator.

A Slower Pace

DC's boutique hotels and cool guesthouses are in the shadier areas of Northwest DC. Guests in these areas will enjoy a slightly slower pace and smaller crowds, and the commute to the Mall and Hill is negligible.

Off season? Not in DC

Summers bring tourists and winters bring policy makers and lobbyists. In fact, when Congress is in session, it's often more expensive to get a room during the week than on the weekend. Your best bet is to head for the suburbs, which are convenient for metro stops.

WHERE THE PRESIDENTS LIVE

In the White House, correct? Not when it's being renovated. George Washington lived in New York and Philadelphia before the Capitol moved to DC. James Madison lived in the Octagon House (18th Street NW and New York Avenue) after the British burned the White House to the ground. Calvin Coolidge hosted Charles Lindbergh at the Patterson House (15 Dupont Circle) while the White House was being renovated. Harry S. Truman moved out for renovations also—to the nearby Blair House at 1651 Pennsylvania Avenue, where two Puerto Rican nationalists tried to assassinate him.

Budget Hotels

ADAMS INN

www.adamsinn.com
This Victorian bed-and-breakfast encompasses three houses on a quiet street near Adams-Morgan. 27 rooms.
🔢 F1 ✉ 1746 Lanier Place NW ☎ 800/578–6807 🚇 Woodley Park–Zoo, then 10-min walk

AMERICANA HOTEL

www.americanahotel.com
Step back in time with a stay in this 102-room hotel whose style is a throwback to the 1960s when it first opened.
🔢 Off map at C9 ✉ 1400 Jefferson Davis Highway, Arlington, VA ☎ 703/979–3772 🚇 Pentagon City/Crystal City

BETHESDA COURT HOTEL

www.bethesdacourtwashdc.com
This three-story inn with an English courtyard serves complimentary afternoon tea. 74 rooms.
🔢 Off map at A1 ✉ 7740 Wisconsin Avenue, Bethesda, MD ☎ 301/656–2100 🚇 Bethesda

CHURCHILL HOTEL

www.thechurchillhotel.com
The Beaux Arts Churchill provides large, comfortable rooms, a helpful staff, valet services and a hilltop view over Dupont Circle.
🔢 E3 ✉ 1914 Connecticut Avenue NW ☎ 202/797–2000; 800/424–2464 reservations 🚇 Dupont Circle

HOTEL HARRINGTON

www.hotel-harrington.com
This is your basic clean, no-frills hotel, but with a great location. The Mall and many museums are just a few blocks away. 242 rooms.
🔢 G6 ✉ 436 11th Street NW ☎ 202/628–8140; 800/424–8532 🚇 Metro Center

HOTEL MADERA

www.hotelmadera.com
A hip boutique hotel attached to a cool restaurant, Madera has large rooms in bold tones. Service is excellent; you can even keep a "stow-away bag" of personal belongings here for your next trip.
🔢 E4 ✉ 1310 New Hampshire Avenue ☎ 202/296–7600 🚇 Dupont Circle

HOTEL TABARD INN

www.tabardinn.com
This charming old inn with plush antique rooms also sports a cozy lounge with a fireplace and a top-notch restaurant.
🔢 F4 ✉ 1739 N Street NW ☎ 202/785–1277 🚇 Dupont Circle

KALORAMA GUEST HOUSE

www.kaloramaguesthouse.com
These Victorian town houses filled with 19th-century furnishings are near the Zoo and Adams-Morgan.
🔢 E2 ✉ 2700 Cathedral Avenue NW ☎ 202/588–8188 🚇 Woodley Park–Zoo

WOODLEY PARK GUEST HOUSE

www.dcinns.com
This intimate bed-and-breakfast near the Zoo has individualized rooms filled with antiques. They are not able to accommodate young children. 15 rooms.
🔢 D1 ✉ 2647 Woodley Road NW ☎ 866/667–0218 🚇 Woodley Park–Zoo

WINDSOR PARK HOTEL

www.windsorparkhotel.com
This charming 43-room hotel in a safe, leafy neighborhood is just a short walk from the Zoo and Rock Creek Park. Free continental breakfast.
🔢 E2 ✉ 2116 Kalorama Road NW ☎ 800/247–3064 🚇 Dupont Circle

Mid-Range Hotels

PRICES

Expect to pay between $175 and $275 per night for a double room in a mid-range hotel.

AKWAABA DC

www.akwaaba.com
A literary-themed luxurious bed-and-breakfast owned by the former editor of *Essence*, Akwaaba sits in a well-located town house.
➕ F3 ✉ 1708 16th Street NW ☎ 866/466–3855
🚇 Dupont Circle

BEACON HOTEL

www.beaconhotelwdc.com
With a popular bar and grill, this lively hotel has well-sized rooms and a steady clientele of business travelers.
➕ F4 ✉ 1615 Rhode Island Avenue NW ☎ 800/821–4367 or 202/296–2100
🚇 Dupont Circle

CAPITOL HILL HOTEL

www.capitolhillhotel-dc.com
Close to the Library of Congress and the Capitol, this collection of tidy suites is home to several members of Congress.
➕ K7 ✉ 200 C Street SE ☎ 202/543–6000 🚇 Capitol South

EMBASSY SUITES

www.embassysuites3.hilton.com
Aside from a magnificent eight-story lush atrium, visitors here enjoy large two-room suites, complimentary breakfast and a free nightly reception.
➕ E4 ✉ 1250 22nd Street NW ☎ 202/857–3388
🚇 Foggy Bottom

THE FAIRFAX AT EMBASSY ROW

www.fairfaxhoteldc.com
On one of Washington's loveliest streets, this former home of Al Gore feels like an old-boys club dressed in late 19th-century furniture.
➕ E3 ✉ 2100 Massachusetts Avenue NW ☎ 202/293–2100
🚇 Dupont Circle

THE GEORGETOWN INN

www.georgetowninn.com
This boutique-style, historic hotel is perfectly located for exploring Georgetown. It offers free internet and has an excellent on-site restaurant.

ARCHITECTURAL GEMS

Even beyond the museums and monuments, DC is replete with architectural eye candy. James Renwick's Smithsonian Castle (1000 Jefferson Drive SW), I. M. Pei's East Building of the National Gallery of Art (▷ 43), John Russell Pope's Scottish Rite Masonic Temple (1733 16th Street NW) and Mies van der Rohe's Martin Luther King, Jr. Library (901 G Street NW) are all worth a look.

➕ C4 ✉ 1310 Wisconsin Avenue NW ☎ 202/333–8900 🚇 Foggy Bottom

THE GRAHAM GEORGETOWN

www.thegrahamgeorgetown.com
This homey hotel offers 57 apartments off a side-street in Georgetown. It retains its high regard for customer service.
➕ D4 ✉ 1075 Thomas Jefferson Street NW ☎ 855/341–1292 🚇 Foggy Bottom, then taxi

HAMPTON INN WASHINGTON-DOWNTOWN-CONVENTION CENTER

http://hamptoninn3.hilton.com
Right in the middle of everything, the Hampton Inn is close to the Metro, the shops and the restaurants of Chinatown, the Convention Center, and music and sports events at the Verizon Center. Free WiFi and an on-site fitness center.
➕ H5 ✉ 901 6th Street NW ☎ 202/842–2500 🚇 Gallery Place–Chinatown

HENLEY PARK HOTEL

www.henleypark.com
A bit of Britain in a developing neighborhood, this Tudor-style hotel is part of the Historic Hotels of America. 96 rooms.
➕ H5 ✉ 926 Massachusetts Avenue NW ☎ 800/222–8474 🚇 Mount Vernon Square, Gallery Place, Metro Center

HOTEL PALOMAR
www.hotelpalomar-dc.com
This arts-themed Kimpton hotel hosts an hour-long wine-tasting every evening. The rooms are large and amenities abound. 335 rooms.
🚇 E4 ✉ 2121 P Street NW ☎ 877/866–3070 🚇 Dupont Circle

HOTEL ROUGE
www.rougehotel.com
Decked out in rich reds and contrasting pale colors, Rouge is distinctly hip and urban. Bar Rouge downstairs draws the same jet set.
🚇 F4 ✉ 1315 16th Street NW ☎ 202/232–8000; 800/738–1202 🚇 Dupont Circle

LIAISON CAPITOL HILL
www.affinia.com/liaison
The Liaison's prime location makes it ideal for visits to many of the major attractions. It has the largest rooftop pool and bar in the city. 340 rooms.
🚇 J6 ✉ 415 New Jersey Avenue NW ☎ 202/638–1616 🚇 Union Station

MARRIOTT WARDMAN PARK
www.marriott.com/WASDT
The huge, brick Victorian hotel looms over the Woodley Park Metro stop, consequently offering a nice view of Rock Creek Park. Amenities abound. 1,052 rooms.
🚇 D1 ✉ 2660 Woodley Road NW ☎ 202/328–2000;

800/228–9290 🚇 Woodley Park–Zoo

MORRISON-CLARK INN HOTEL
www.morrisonclark.com
Created by merging two 1864 town houses, this 54-room inn, part of the Historic Hotels of America, has individually decorated, colonial rooms.
🚇 G4 ✉ 1015 L Street NW ☎ 202/898–1200; 800/332–7898 🚇 Mount Vernon Square

THE NORMANDY HOTEL
www.thenormandydc.com
This European-style hotel, on a quiet embassy-lined street, is popular among diplomats. There's a wine and cheese reception every Tuesday evening. Use of a health club at a sister hotel. 75 rooms.
🚇 E2 ✉ 2118 Wyoming Avenue NW ☎ 202/483–1350 🚇 Dupont Circle

HOTEL WITH ATTITUDE

Heavily evoking 1960s Hollywood glamor with a touch of Nintendo, the Helix, one of DC's coolest hotels, is also situated in one of DC's up-and-coming neighborhoods, Logan Circle. 175 rooms.
🚇 G4 ✉ 1430 Rhode Island Avenue NW ☎ 202/462–9001; 800/706–1202, www.hotelhelix.com 🚇 Dupont Circle

---

THE QUINCY
www.thequincy.com
These well-located suites offer quick access to the White House, Dupont Circle and Downtown.
🚇 F4 ✉ 1823 L Street NW ☎ 202/223–4320 🚇 Farragut North

RIVER INN
www.theriverinn.com
This small, all-suite hotel is near Georgetown, George Washington University and the John F. Kennedy Center. Rooms are homey if modest. 126 rooms.
🚇 D5 ✉ 924 25th Street NW ☎ 202/337–7600 🚇 Foggy Bottom

SWANN HOUSE
www.swannhouse.com
Converted from an 1883 Dupont Circle mansion, this bed-and-breakfast wows with feather beds, chandeliers and original molding.
🚇 F3 ✉ 1808 New Hampshire Avenue NW ☎ 202/265–4414 🚇 Dupont Circle

TOPAZ HOTEL
www.topazhotel.com
Bright earthy stripes and polka dots grace the walls and fabrics here at this "wellness"-themed hotel, which serves energy shakes in the morning. The large rooms contain a bed, desk, settee and dressing room.
🚇 F4 ✉ 1733 N Street NW ☎ 202/393–3000; 800/775–1202 🚇 Dupont Circle

Luxury Hotels

PRICES

Expect to pay more than $275 per night for a double room in a luxury hotel.

FOUR SEASONS HOTEL

www.fourseasons.com/washington
A gathering place for Washington's elite, this hotel features custom-made furniture and stunning artwork in all the rooms from the deluxe to the Royal Suite. 222 rooms.

➕ D4 ✉ 2800 Pennsylvania Avenue NW ☎ 202/342–0444 Ⓜ Foggy Bottom

HAY-ADAMS HOTEL

www.hayadams.com
Looking like a mansion on the outside and an English country house within, this hotel has a picture-postcard White House view—ask for a room on the south side. 145 rooms.

➕ F5 ✉ 800 16th Street NW ☎ 202/638–6600 Ⓜ McPherson Square

HOTEL MONACO

www.monaco-dc.com
Built in 1839 by the designer of the Washington Monument, Monaco has rooms with vaulted ceilings around a landscaped courtyard.

➕ H5 ✉ 700 F Street NW ☎ 800/649–1202; 202/628–7177 Ⓜ Gallery Place–Chinatown

MANDARIN ORIENTAL

www.mandarinoriental.com/washington
This large modern hotel, with 400 rooms and a short walk from the Tidal Basin, features subdued rooms with an Asian flare. You'll find the restaurants, Muze (▷ 52) and Empress Lounge are popular.

➕ H7 ✉ 1330 Maryland Avenue SW ☎ 202/554–8588 Ⓜ Smithsonian

MANSION ON O STREET

www.omansion.com
Popular among the jet set, this group of Victorian town houses offers luxurious and creatively themed rooms. A hotel with a difference.

➕ E4 ✉ 2020 O Street NW ☎ 202/496–2000 Ⓜ Dupont Circle

BOOKING AGENCIES

Capitol Reservations

Book rooms online at more than 70 hotels and inns at 20–40 percent off certain rates. www.capitolreservations.com

Destination DC

A resource for finding hotels (both chain and boutique style), bed-and-breakfasts and campgrounds in the DC area. Either book online or call toll-free.

☎ 800/422–8644; www.washington.org

RENAISSANCE MAYFLOWER

www.marriott.com
The lobby of this grand hotel glistens with gilded trim. The rooms have hosted many presidents, celebrities and royalty.

➕ F4 ✉ 1127 Connecticut Avenue NW ☎ 202/347–3000; 800/228–7697 Ⓜ Farragut North

RITZ-CARLTON, GEORGETOWN

www.ritzcarlton.com/georgetown
Housed in the former Georgetown incinerator, this sleek hotel is luxurious and cozy.

➕ C4 ✉ 3100 South Street NW ☎ 202/912–4100 Ⓜ Foggy Bottom

SOFITEL, LAFAYETTE SQUARE

www.sofitelwashingtondc.com
This Jazz-Age hotel caters to an international clientele. Enjoy one of the 237 chic rooms and world-class food at Ici Urban Bistro.

➕ G5 ✉ 806 15th Street NW ☎ 202/730–8800 Ⓜ McPherson Square

WILLARD INTERCONTINENTAL

www.washington.intercontinental.com
Heads of state have made the Willard Intercontinental their home since 1853. The lobby is Beaux Arts.

➕ G5 ✉ 1401 Pennsylvania Avenue NW ☎ 202/628–9100 Ⓜ Metro Center

This section contains essential information about preparing for your journey to Washington, how to get around once you are there, and other practicalities.

Planning Ahead

When to Go

There is no bad time to visit Washington. Spring is busiest, when the city's cherry trees are in blossom. October and November bring brilliant foliage. Summer, although crowded and sweltering, sees a chockablock calendar of special events, many of which are free.

TIME

Washington is on Eastern Standard Time. Clocks go forward one hour in March and back in late October.

AVERAGE DAILY MAXIMUM TEMPERATURES

	JAN	FEB	MAR	APR	MAY	JUN	JUL	AUG	SEP	OCT	NOV	DEC
°F	42°F	45°F	53°F	64°F	75°F	83°F	87°F	84°F	78°F	67°F	55°F	45°F
°C	6°C	7°C	12°C	18°C	24°C	28°C	31°C	29°C	26°C	19°C	13°C	7°C

Spring (mid-March to May) is extremely pleasant, with flowers and trees in bloom throughout the city.

Summer (June to early September) is hot and humid, with temperatures sometimes reaching 95°F (35°C) or more.

Fall (mid-September to November) is comfortable, and sometimes bracing.

Winter (December to mid-March) varies from year to year: It can be extremely cold or surprisingly warm. The occasional snowfall shuts the city down.

WHAT'S ON

January *Antiques Show* (washingtonwintershow.com).
Martin Luther King, Jr. Birthday Observations.
Restaurant Week (ramw.org/restaurantweek).
February *Presidents' Day.*
Chinese New Year's Parade (sometimes takes place in January).
March *St. Patrick's Day Festival* (www.shamrockfest.com).
Organist's Bach Marathon.
Blossom Kite Festival.
April *National Cherry Blossom Festival*

(www.nationalcherry blossomfestival.org).
White House Spring Garden Tour (www.whitehouse.org).
Filmfest DC (www.film festdc.org).
May *Washington National Cathedral Flower Mart.*
Memorial Day Concert.
June *Capital Pride Festival* (www.capitalpride.org).
Military Band Summer Concert Series (www.aoc.gov).
July *Smithsonian Folklife Festival* (www.festival.si.edu).
Independence Day (Jul 4, www.nps.gov).

September *National Symphony Orchestra Labor Day Concert* (www.kennedy-center.org).
Adams-Morgan Day.
October *Marine Corps Marathon* (www.marinemarathon.com).
Taste of DC Festival (www.thetasteofdc.org).
November *Veterans' Day.*
December *National Christmas Tree Lighting* (www.thenationaltree.org).
You can find information about events in the area on the travel site http://washington.org.

Washington Online

www.si.edu
The Smithsonian Institution site features a directory of its 18 museums, schedules of events and exhibits, information about research and publications and a link to the gift shop.

http://washington.org
This site is presented by the Washington DC, Convention and Tourism board. You can make hotel reservations, gather information about the different neighborhoods and find out about annual events.

www.culturaltourismdc.org
The website of this nonprofit coalition of DC cultural and neighborhood organizations hosts comprehensive and easy-to-navigate listings of DC districts, walks, events and attractions that you might not be able to find elsewhere.

www.washingtonflyer.com
The online hub of *Washington Flyer*, the official magazine of the Metropolitan Washington Airports Authority, is a solid resource on flying in and out of DC.

www.opentable.com
Allows diners to check availability and make reservations at most Washington restaurants.

www.washingtonpost.com
The newspaper's site features a Going Out guide, including airport status reports, calendar of events and reviews of nightlife and restaurants.

www.washingtoncitypaper.com
The site of this alternative weekly carries the newspaper's superb arts coverage as well as a "Restaurant Finder," with reviews from the paper's critics and visitors to the site.

www.senate.gov and www.house.gov
Congress website including information on upcoming votes, history and how to visit.

TRAVEL SITES

www.fodors.com
A complete travel-planning site. You can research prices and weather; book air tickets, cars and rooms; ask questions (and get answers) from fellow travelers; and find links to other sites.

www.wmata.com
The Washington Metropolitan Area Transit Authority site features maps of the Metro and bus systems, plus information on delays and vacation schedules.

Getting There

BUS TRAVEL

Several bus companies—some with free WiFi and onboard movies—pick up passengers throughout Washington and offer inexpensive rides to New York. Try www.bestbus.com or www.boltbus.com.

TRAIN TRAVEL

Amtrak (www.amtrack. com) trains leave on tracks stretching out the back of Union Station. Service to New York takes 3–4 hours; it's almost 8 hours to Boston. The high-speed Acela cuts journeys down to less than 3 hours and 6.5 hours respectively. Two less-expensive commuter lines service the Virginia and Maryland suburbs on weekdays.

VISAS FOR USA

Visitors traveling on a full British passport are required to obtain an electronic authorization to travel. Go to the official US government website https://esta.cbp.dhs.gov to apply and pay a visa fee of US$14 by credit card.

AIRPORTS

Flying time to Washington, DC, is 1 hour 15 minutes from New York, 5 hours 40 minutes from Los Angeles and 6 hours 45 minutes from London. The major airports include Reagan National Airport, Dulles International Airport and Baltimore-Washington International Airport (BWI).

FROM REAGAN NATIONAL AIRPORT

Reagan National Airport (tel 703/417– 8000, www.metwashairports.com) is in Virginia, 4 miles (6.4km) south of Downtown and the closest to central Washington. A taxi to Downtown takes about 20 minutes and costs around $15–$25. SuperShuttle (tel 800/258–3826, www.supershuttle.com) offers an airport-to-door service for $14 per person 24 hours a day. The blue and yellow Metro lines run from the airport to Downtown, with stations next to terminals B and C (Mon–Thu 5am–midnight, Fri 5am–3am, Sat 7am–3am, Sun 7am–midnight). Fare cards ($3.30) can be bought from machines on level 2 near the pedestrian bridges linking the two terminals. For Metro information call 202/637–7000.

RMA (tel 800/878–7743) will arrange for a car or limousine to meet you at the airport. Cost is around $150 for a sedan and $350 for a limousine, plus a 20 percent tip.

FROM DULLES INTERNATIONAL AIRPORT

Dulles International Airport (tel 703/572–2700, www.mwaa.com/dulles) is 26 miles (42km)

west of Washington. A taxi to the city takes around 40 minutes and costs around $65. The Washington Flyer Coach (tel 888/927–4359) goes from the airport to the Wiehle–Reston East Metro. Buses leave the airport every 15–20 minutes Mon–Fri 6am–10.40pm, Sat–Sun 7.45am–10.45pm. The 10-minute trip costs $5 ($10 round-trip). SuperShuttle (tel 800/258–3826) costs $29 per person, plus $10 for each additional person. RMA (tel 800/878–7743) costs around $150 for a sedan and $350 for a limousine, plus a 20 percent gratuity.

FROM BWI AIRPORT

Baltimore-Washington International Airport (tel 800/435–9294, www.bwiairport.com) is in Maryland, 30 miles (48km) northeast of Washington. A taxi from the airport takes around 45 minutes and costs $90. SuperShuttle (tel 800/258–3826) costs $37, plus $12 for each additional person. Free shuttle buses run between airline terminals and the train station. Amtrak (tel 800/872–7245, www.amtrak.com) and MARC (tel 866/743–3682, www.mta.maryland.gov) trains run between the airport and Union Station. The 40-minute ride costs $15–$41 (depending on day and time) on Amtrak and $6 on MARC (weekdays only). With RMA you'll pay $150 for a sedan or $350 for a limousine, plus a 20 percent gratuity.

INSURANCE

Check your policy and buy any necessary supplements. It is vital that travel insurance covers medical expenses, in addition to accident, trip cancellation, baggage loss and theft. Also make sure the policy covers any continuing treatment for a more chronic condition.

ENTRY REQUIREMENTS

For the latest passport and visa information, look up the embassy website at www.usembassy.org.uk. The authorities are now subjecting more people to even more security checks. To avoid problems allow plenty of time for clearing security, and be sure to check the latest advice. See also panel opposite.

AIRLINES

Major air carriers serving the three airports (Reagan National Airport, Dulles International Airport and Baltimore-Washington International Airport) include:

Air Canada	☎ 888/247–2262
Air France	☎ 800/321–4538
British Airways	☎ 800/247–9297
Continental	☎ 800/523–3273
Delta	☎ 404/773–0305
El Al	☎ 800/223–6700
Frontier Airlines	☎ 800/432–1359
Icelandair	☎ 800/223–5500
Japan Airlines	☎ 800/525–3663
KLM Royal Dutch	☎ 866/434–0320
Lufthansa	☎ 800/645–3880
Saudi Arabian Airlines	☎ 800/472–8342
United	☎ 800/864–8331
US Airways	☎ 866/428–4322
Virgin Atlantic	☎ 800/862–8621

For less expensive flights, contact:
Southwest Airlines ☎ 800/435–9792,
Spirit Airlines ☎ 801/401–2200 or
JetBlue Airways ☎ 800/538–2583.

Getting Around

VISITORS WITH DISABILITIES

Museums and other public buildings are often equipped with ramps and elevators and are usually accessible to wheelchair users. Wheelchair access to Metro trains is via elevators from street level; details at www.wmata.com. Information on various DC locations can be found on individual websites.

SPEEDING

Should you decide to drive in DC, don't exceed the speed limits. There are hidden cameras in popular areas that will take photos of your plates and send you a fine.

PUBLIC TRANSPORTATION

● The subway (Metro) and bus (Metrobus) systems are run by the Washington Metropolitan Area Transit Authority (WMATA).
● Maps of the Metro system and some bus schedules are available in all Metro stations or at WMATA headquarters (600 5th Street NW).
● For general information call 202/637–7000, open Mon–Fri 6am–8.30pm, Sat–Sun 7am–8.30pm, www.wmata.com.
● The WMATA website is updated throughout the day showing problems on individual routes.
● Lost and Found (tel 202/962–1195); Transit police (tel 202/962–2121).

BUSES

● Bus signs are blue and red and white.
● The bus system covers a much wider area than the Metro. The fare within the city is $1.75.
● Free bus-to-bus transfers are available when using a SmarTrip card and are good for about 2 hours at designated Metrobus transfer points.
● A 7-day regional SmarTrip bus pass costs $17.50.

METRO

● The city's subway system, the Metro, is one of the cleanest and safest in the country. You need a farecard to ride, called a SmarTrip card, both to enter and exit the train area. Farecard machines, located in the stations, take coins and $1, $5, $10 and $20 notes. The most change the machine will give you is about $10, so don't use a large bill if you are buying a low-value card.
● Metro stations are marked by tall brown pillars with a large, white "M" at the top. A colored stripe under the "M" indicates the line or lines that are serviced by the station.
● Trains run every few minutes on Mon–Thu 5am–midnight; Fri 5am–3am; Sat 7am–3am; Sun 7am–midnight.
● The basic peak fare ($2.15) increases based on the length of your trip. It is cheaper at off-peak times. Maps in stations tell you both

the rush-hour fare and regular fare to any destination station. A one-day pass is $14.50.

● Insert your farecard into the slot on the front of the turnstile. Retrieve it once the gate opens as you will need it to exit. If you have a SmarTrip card tap it on the fare gate on entry and exit.

● Transfer to a bus upon leaving the Metro. The ability to transfer to a bus from the Metro is only available if you have a SmartTrip card.

DC CIRCULATOR

● An alternative to the Metro, the large red buses of the DC Circulator run every 10 minutes on five routes connecting places of interest and cost only $1. Routes: Dupont Circle–Georgetown–Rosslyn; Georgetown–Union Station; Potomac Avenue Metro–Skyland; Union Station–Navy Yard; Woodley Park–Adams Morgan–McPherson Square. Full details of the routes and operating hours can be found on the website (www.dccirculator.com).

TAXIS

● Taxis are abundant and safe in Washington. Look for cars with white lights on their roof tops, which signals they are open. Fares are $3.25 upon entering the cab and 27 cents for each additional one eighth of a mile. Other charges that may be added include luggage at $0.50 a piece; if you're coming from the airport, there's an additional charge of $3; each additional passenger is $1.

DRIVING

● Driving in Washington is for the patient only.

● Although "right turn on red" is permitted, most Downtown intersections have signs forbidding it from 7am–7pm, or banning it outright. Virginia also allows "left turn on red" when turning into a one-way street from another one-way street.

● The speed limit in the city varies from street to street; the maximum speed limit in residential areas is 25mph (40kph).

● Seat belts are mandatory.

CAR RENTAL

Alamo ☎ 800/028–2390
Avis ☎ 800/633–3469
Budget ☎ 800/218–7992
Dollar ☎ 800/800–4000
Hertz ☎ 800/654–3131
National ☎ 877/222–9058

You will have to provide a credit card and drivers under 25 years old may have to pay a local surcharge.

PARKING IN DC

Parking is a problem in Washington, as the public parking areas fill up quickly with local workers' cars. If you park on city streets, check the signs to make sure it is permitted: Green and white signs show when parking is allowed, red and white signs when it is not. Parking on most main streets is not permitted during rush hours, and if you park illegally your car is likely to get towed. If it does, call ☎ 202/737–4404 to find out where it is and how to get it back. If it is towed on a weekend (after 7pm Friday) you'll have to wait until Monday to retrieve it.

Essential Facts

MONEY

The unit of currency is the dollar (= 100 cents). Notes (bills) come in denominations of $1, $5, $10, $20, $50 and $100; coins come in 25¢ (a quarter), 10¢ (a dime), 5¢ (a nickel) and 1¢ (a penny). Sales tax in Washington, DC, is 5.75 percent, hotel tax 14.5 percent (varies in Virginia) and food and beverage tax 10 percent.

CUSTOMS

● Visitors aged 21 or over may import duty free: 200 cigarettes or 100 cigars; 1 liter (1 US quart) of alcohol; and gifts up to $100 in value.

● Restricted import items include meat, seeds, plants and fruit.

● Some medication bought over the counter abroad may be prescription-only in the US and may be confiscated. Bring a doctor's certificate for essential medication.

ELECTRICITY

● The electricity supply is 110 volts AC, and plugs are standard two pins. Foreign visitors will need an adaptor and voltage converter for their own appliances.

EMBASSIES AND CONSULATES

● Canada at 501 Pennsylvania Avenue NW (tel 202/682–1740, www.can-am.gc.ca/washington).

● Ireland at 2234 Massachusetts Avenue NW (tel 202/462–3939, www.embassyofireland.org).

● UK at 3100 Massachusetts Avenue NW (tel 202/588–6500, www.gov.uk/government/world/organisations/british-embassy-washington).

EMERGENCY PHONE NUMBERS

● Police 911
● Fire 911
● Ambulance 911
● For all other non-urgent matters 311.

LOST PROPERTY

● Metro or Metrobus tel 202/962–1195
● Smithsonian museums tel 202/633–5630
● Other lost articles, call the city on 311.

MAIL

● The North Capitol Station has the longest hours at 2 Massachusetts Avenue NE (tel 202/636–1259, open Mon–Fri 9–7, Sat–Sun 9–5).

Other branches are at:
- Farragut, 1800 M Street NW, tel 202/636–1259, Mon–Fri 9–5
- L'Enfant Plaza, 470 L'Enfant Plaza SW, tel 202/268–4970, Mon–Fri 8–5
- Washington Square, 1050 Connecticut Avenue NW, tel 202/636–1259, Mon–Fri 9–5
- Union Station, 50 Massachsetts Avenue NE, tel 202/636–1259, Mon–Fri 7.30–5, Sat 7.30–3.30.

MEDICAL TREATMENT
- The hospital closest to Downtown is George Washington University Hospital (900 23rd Street NW, tel 202/715–4000). Try Inn House Doctor for urgent care visits to Washington DC hotels (tel 202/216–9100).
- The DC Dental Society operates an online referral service (www.dcdental.org).
- CVS operates 24-hour pharmacies at 6514 Georgia Avenue (tel 202/829–5234) and 6 Dupont Circle NW (tel 202/785–1466).

MONEY MATTERS
- Credit cards are widely accepted in hotels, restaurants and shops, but some retailers may impose a surcharge.
- Tipping is expected for all services. As a guide the following applies:
Restaurants 15–20 percent
Bartenders 15 percent per round of drinks
Hairdressers 15 percent
Taxis 15 percent
Chambermaids $1 per day
Porters $1 per bag.

NEWSPAPERS AND MAGAZINES
- Washington has two major daily newspapers, *The Washington Post* and *The Washington Times*, which is more conservative.
- The *City Paper*, a free weekly with an emphasis on entertainment, is available from newspaper boxes around town and at many restaurants, clubs and other outlets (www.washingtoncitypaper.com).

STREET NAMES

Washington's street names are based on a quadrant system, the center of which is the Capitol building. Numbered streets run north–south, while lettered streets run east–west. Both progress with distance from the Capitol. There is no "J" Street, eliminated to prevent confusion with "I" Street. For example, 1900 R Street NW is 19 blocks west and 17 blocks north of the Capitol, as "R" is the 17th letter if you skip "J." Diagonal avenues cut across the grid. They are named after the States based on their date of statehood and their proximity to the Capitol. Delaware, the "First State," is closest.

TOILETS

It's best to use those in large hotels and stores, galleries and museums.

RADIO

- FM Radio 88.5 (WAMU)—National Public Radio (news)
- 90.9 (WETA)—Classical
- 98.7 (WMZQ)—Country
- 99.5 (WIHT)—Pop
- 101.1 (WWDC)—Rock
- 107.3 (WRQX)—Adult Contemporary

LOCAL BLOGS

- dc.eater.com/—the place for foodies, area restaurant news and reviews.
- www.dcist.com—thorough news and goings-on site.
- www.washingtonpost.com/goingoutguide—postings by the Washington Post's team of entertainment experts.

- In addition, various neighborhood weekly newspapers serve Capitol Hill, Georgetown, Adams-Morgan and other areas.
- *Washingtonian*, a monthly magazine, has a calendar of events, dining information, arts reviews and articles about the city and its prominent people.
- *Where/Washington*, a monthly magazine listing popular things to do, is free at most hotels.
- Other national newspapers are available.

OPENING HOURS

- Stores generally open Mon–Sat 10–6; Sun 12–5.
- Banks open Mon–Fri 9–5, although hours can vary.
- Post offices open Mon–Fri 8–5, with some offices open Sat.

PUBLIC HOLIDAYS

- Jan 1: New Year's Day
- Third Mon in Jan: Birthday of Martin Luther King, Jr.
- Third Mon in Feb: Presidents' Day
- Last Mon in May: Memorial Day
- Jul 4: Independence Day
- First Mon in Sep: Labor Day
- Second Mon in Oct: Columbus Day
- Nov 11: Veterans Day
- Fourth Thu in Nov: Thanksgiving Day
- Dec 25: Christmas Day
- On public holidays banks and post offices close while many stores and restaurants stay open.

SMOKING

DC is becoming less and less friendly to those who want to light up. Smoking is banned in almost all indoor public places, including restaurants, bars and clubs.

STATE REGULATIONS

- You must be 21 years old to drink alcohol in Washington, and you may be required to produce proof of age and photo ID.

STUDENTS

● Holders of an International Student Identity Card may be entitled to discounts at some clothing and electronic stores, theaters, cinemas and restaurants.

VISITOR INFORMATION

● Destination DC is at 901 7th Street NW, 4th Floor, Washington, DC, 20001 (tel 202/789–7000, www.washington.org).

● Tourist Information is at 506 9th Street NW (tel 866/324–7386, www.downtowndc.org, Mon–Fri 8.30–5.30).

● National Park Service is at 1849 C Street NW, Washington DC 20240 (tel 202/208–3818, www.nps.gov).

● National Park Service information kiosks can be found on the Mall, near the White House, next to the Vietnam Veterans Memorial and at several other locations throughout the city.

● The White House Visitor Center is located at Baldridge Hall in the Department of Commerce Building, 1450 Pennsylvania Avenue NW (tel 202/208–1631, www.nps.gov/whho, open daily 7.30–4.

● For recorded information on exhibits and special offerings at Smithsonian Institution museums, tel 202/633–1000.

● Discounted tickets for the theater, concerts, ballet, opera, cinema and galleries can be found at Ticketplace (www.ticketplace.org).

WASHINGTON SLANG

● "Hill staffers"—staff for individual members of Congress who work on Capitol Hill. Dominant demographic in DC.

● "Inside the Beltway"—the "Beltway"(I–495) forms a circle around the District. This refers to the American political system and its insularity.

● "Foggy Bottom," "Langley"—agencies are often referred to by their location. These are the State Department and CIA, respectively.

● "NoVa"—short for "Northern Virginia," this typically refers to Arlington and Alexandria. Occasionally used as a term of derision.

TELEPHONES

● To call Washington from the UK, dial 00 1, Washington's area code (202), and then the number.
● To call the UK from Washington, dial 011 44, then omit the first zero from the area code.

SAFETY

Washington is as safe as any large city, but the usual commonsense rules apply. Because of the wide income divide, crime statistics vary hugely from block to block. Tourist areas that are safe during the day may not be safe at night. At night walk with someone rather than alone; use taxis in less populous areas.

NEED TO KNOW ESSENTIAL FACTS

Timeline

EARLY DAYS

In 1779, President George Washington was authorized by Congress to build a Federal City. The following year, he hired Pierre Charles L'Enfant to design a city beside the Potomac River. According to legend, he sited the US Capitol in the exact middle of the 13 original states. By 1800, President Adams was able to occupy the unfinished White House, and Congress met in the Capitol, also unfinished. The population was by then around 3,000.

DOWN THE WIRE

In 1844, Samuel F. B. Morse transmitted the first telegraph message from the Capitol to Baltimore, Maryland.

1812 The US declares war on Britain in response to the impressment of sailors from American ships and border disputes in Canada.

1814 The British sack Washington, burning the White House and the Capitol. The war ends with the Treaty of Ghent, ratified in late 1814.

1846 Congress accepts James Smithson's bequest and establishes the Smithsonian Institution.

1850 The slave trade is abolished in the District of Columbia.

1863 President Abraham Lincoln's Emancipation Proclamation frees the nation's slaves; many move to Washington.

1865 Lincoln is assassinated during a performance at Ford's Theatre.

1867 Howard University is chartered by Congress to educate blacks.

1876 The nation's centennial is celebrated with a fair in Philadelphia.

1901 The McMillan Commission oversees the city's beautification.

1907 Trains run to the new Union Station.

1922 The Lincoln Memorial is completed, 57 years after Lincoln's death.

1943 The Jefferson Memorial and Pentagon are completed.

1961 President John F. Kennedy plans the renovation of Pennsylvania Avenue. Residents are given the right to vote in presidential elections.

1974 The Watergate Hotel becomes infamous as the site of the bungled Republican robbery attempt on Democratic headquarters. President Nixon resigns as a result of the ensuing cover-up.

1981 President Ronald Reagan is shot outside the Washington Hilton.

1991 Mayor Sharon Pratt Dixon Kelly becomes the first African American to lead a major US city.

2001 Terrorists highjack a passenger plane from Dulles Airport on September 11 and crash it into the Pentagon, killing many people.

2009 Barack Obama, the first African-American president, is inaugurated.

2011 The Martin Luther King, Jr. Memorial is dedicated to the civil rights leader.

2012 Groundbreaking ceremony for the Smithsonian's National Museum of African-American History and Culture, with a projected opening date of 2016.

2015 District Councilwoman Muriel Bowser is sworn in as the seventh mayor of DC.

"I HAVE A DREAM"

On August 28, 1963, Martin Luther King, Jr. delivered his vision of racial harmony from the steps of the Lincoln Memorial to a crowd of 200,000. Born in 1929, King had entered the ministry in 1955. As pastor of the Dexter Avenue Baptist Church in Montgomery, Alabama, he became the figurehead of the organized non-violent civil-rights protests to end discrimination laws. His "I Have a Dream" speech ended a march on Washington by blacks and whites calling for reform. King was awarded the Nobel Peace Prize in 1964. His last sermon was at Washington National Cathedral in 1968—he was shot five days later in Memphis.

Below from left to right: Martin Luther King, Jr.; Smithsonian Institute; Union Station; Vietnam Memorial; George Washington

Index

Washington, D.C. 25 Best

WRITTEN BY Mary Case and Bruce Walker
ADDITIONAL WRITING BY Matthew Cordell
UPDATED BY Anita Sach
SERIES EDITOR Clare Ashton
COVER DESIGN Chie Ushio, Yuko Inagaki
DESIGN WORK Tracey Butler
IMAGE RETOUCHING AND REPRO Jacqueline Street-Elkayam

Published in the United Kingdom by AA Publishing

ISBN 978-1-1018-7951-1

TENTH EDITION

All details in this book are based on information supplied to us at press time. Always confirm information when it matters, especially if you're making a detour to visit a specific place. Fodor's expressly disclaims any liability, loss, or risk, personal or otherwise, that is incurred as a consequence of the use of any of the contents of this book.

SPECIAL SALES
This book is available for special discounts for bulk purchases for sales promotions or premiums. For more information, email specialmarkets@randomhouse.com.

Color separation by AA Digital Department
Printed and bound by Leo Paper Products, China

10 9 8 7 6 5 4 3 2 1

A05314
Maps in this title produced from mapping © MAIRDUMONT / Falk Verlag 2013
Transport map © Communicarta Ltd, UK

The Automobile Association would like to thank the following photographers, companies and picture libraries for their assistance in the preparation of this book:

2 AA/C Sawyer; 3 AA/C Sawyer; 4t AA/C Sawyer; 4l AA/C Sawyer; 5t AA/C Sawyer; 5c AA/C Sawyer; 6t AA/C Sawyer; 6cl AA/C Sawyer; 6c AA/C Sawyer; 6cr AA/C Sawyer; 6bl AA/C Sawyer; 6bc AA/C Sawyer; 6br AA/E Davies; 7t AA/C Sawyer; 7tl AA/C Sawyer; 7tc AA/E Davies; 7tr AA/C Sawyer; 7bl AA/E Davies; 7bc AA/E Davies; 7br AA/C Sawyer; 8t AA/C Sawyer; 9t AA/C Sawyer; 10t AA/C Sawyer; 10tr AA/C Sawyer; 10ct AA/C Sawyer; 10cb AA/C Sawyer; 10b AA/E Davies; 11t AA/C Sawyer; 11l AA/C Sawyer; 11ct AA/M Jourdan; 11cb AA/H Harris; 11b AA/C Sawyer; 12t AA/C Sawyer; 13t AA/C Sawyer; 13tl Brand X Pics;13ct AA/C Sawyer;13c Digital Vision; 13cb Digital Vision; 13b RosalreneBetancourt1/Alamy; 14t AA/C Sawyer; 14tr AA/C Sawyer; 14ct AA/J Love; 14cb ImageState; 14b AA/J Love; 15t AA/C Sawyer; 16tr AA/J Love; 16t AA/C Sawyer; 16cr AA/J Love; 16br AA/J Love; 17t AA/C Sawyer; 17tl Image 100; 17ctl AA/J Love; 17cbl AA/J Love; 17b StockByte; 18t AA/J Love; 18tr AA/C Sawyer; 18ctr AA/C Sawyer; 18cbr AA/J Love; 18br AA/J Love; 19t AA/C Sawyer; 19ct AA/C Sawyer; 19c AA/E Davies; 19cbt AA/C Sawyer; 19cb courtesy of Rock Creek Park; 19b AA/J Holmes; 20/1 AA/C Sawyer; 24l AA/J Love; 24r Richard T. Nowitz/CORBIS; 25 AA/E Davies; 26t AA/C Sawyer; 26b K. L. Howard/Alamy; 27t AA/C Sawyer; 27b AA/J Love; 28 AA/C Sawyer; 29t AA/H Harris; 30 PhotoDisc; 31 AA/J Tims; 32 BananaStock; 33 AA/C Sawyer; 36l Blaine Harrington III/Alamy; 36r AA/E Davies; 37 AA/J Love; 38l AA/C Sawyer; 38c AA/C Sawyer; 38r AA/C Sawyer; 39l joeysworld.com / Alamy; 39r RGB Ventures LLC dba SuperStock/Alamy; 40/41 AA/J Love; 41 David R. Frazier Photolibrary, Inc./Alamy; 42 K. L. Howard/Alamy; 42r AA/E Davies; 43l AA/J Love; 43r David Coleman/ Alamy; 44l AA/J Love; 44c AA/J Love; 44r AA/J Love; 45l AA/J Love; 45c AA/J Love; 45r AA/J Love; 46l AA/C Sawyer; 46/7tc AA/C Sawyer; 46/47bc AA/C Sawyer; 47l AA/E Davies; 47r AA/C Sawyer; 48l AA/C Sawyer; 48r AA/C Sawyer; 49t AA/C Sawyer; 49b AA/C Sawyer; 50t AA/C Sawyer; 50bl AA/E Davies; 50br AA/E Davies; 51 AA/C Sawyer; 52t Digital Vision; 52c AA/D Corrance; 53 AA/C Sawyer; 56 AA/C Sawyer; 57l AA/E Davies; 57r AA/C Sawyer; 58 AA/E Davies; 58/9 AA/E Davies; 60l AA/C Sawyer; 60/1tc AA/C Sawyer; 60/61bc AA/C Sawyer; 61l AA/C Sawyer; 61r AA/C Sawyer; 62 AA/J Love; 63l AA/C Sawyer; 63r AA/C Sawyer; 64 Andre Jenny/Alamy; 65 AA/C Sawyer; 66 AA/C Sawyer; 67 PhotoDisc; 68 AA/P Bennett; 69 AA/J Love; 72 AA/C Sawyer; 73l AA/C Sawyer; 73r AA/C Sawyer; 74l AA/C Sawyer; 74r AA/C Sawyer; 75t AA/C Sawyer; 75bl AA/E Davies; 75br Lee Foster/Alamy; 76 AA/C Sawyer; 77 AA/E Davies; 78 Digital Vision; 79 LOOK Die Bildagentur der Fotografen GmbH/Alamy; 80 AA/C Sawyer; 81 AA/C Sawyer; 84l AA/E Davies; 84r AA/E Davies; 85 courtesy of Phillips Collection; 86l courtesy of Rock Creek Park; 86r courtesy of Rock Creek Park; 87l AA/J Love; 87r AA/J Love; 88t AA/C Sawyer; 89 AA/C Sawyer; 90 AA/C Sawyer; 91 AA/C Sawyer; 92 Brand X Pics; 93 AA/P Bennett; 94 Brand X Pics; 95 AA/J Love; 98 AA/C Sawyer; 98/9t AA/C Sawyer; 98/9c AA/E Davies; 99r AA/E Davies; 100l AA/E Davies; 100r AA/C Sawyer; 101 AA/J Love; 102t AA/C Sawyer; 102bl AA/N Ray; 102br AA/J Love; 103t AA/E Davies; 103bl AA/E Davies; 103br AA/E Davies; 104 AA/S McBride; 105 Digital Vision; 106 AA/C Sawyer; 107 AA/J Love; 108t AA/C Sawyer; 108tr PhotoDisc; 108ct AA/C Sawyer; 108cb PhotoDisc; 108b PhotoDisc; 109 AA/C Sawyer; 110 AA/C Sawyer; 111 AA/C Sawyer; 112 AA/C Sawyer; 113 AA/C Sawyer; 114 AA/C Sawyer; 115 AA/C Sawyer; 116 AA/C Sawyer; 117 AA/C Sawyer; 118t AA/C Sawyer; 118b AA/E Davies; 119t AA/C Sawyer; 119b AA/E Davies; 120 AA/C Sawyer; 121 AA/C Sawyer; 122t AA/C Sawyer; 123 AA/C Sawyer; 124t AA/C Sawyer; 124bl Hulton Archive/Getty Images; 124bc AA/C Sawyer; 124/5b AA/E Davies; 125t AA/C Sawyer; 125bc AA/C Sawyer; 125br AA/AA.

Every effort has been made to trace the copyright holders, and we apologize in advance for any unintentional omissions or errors. We would be pleased to apply any corrections in a following edition of this publication.

Titles in the Series